Anglo-Saxon
Poems, Charms, and Proverbs

Old English Text, Translation, and Word List

Matthew Leigh Embleton
www.matthewleighembleton.co.uk

1st Edition

Anglo-Saxon Poems, Charms, and Prove~

Cover: Anglo-Saxon text over an outline of England
Source: Author's design

3

Acknowledgments

I have long been fascinated by languages and history, and I am very grateful to the special people in my life who have supported and encouraged me in my work. Thank you for believing in me. You know who you are.

Introduction

Old English (*Ænglisc*) is the earliest recorded form of the English language. As a West Germanic language, it was brought to Great Britain by Anglo-Saxon settlers in the mid-5th century, and the first literary works date from the mid 7th century.

'Chronicle Poems' found in the Anglo-Saxon Chronicles comment on significant events such as *The Capture of the Five Boroughs*, *The Coronation of Edgar*, and *The Death of Edward (the Confessor)*.

'Metrical Charms' contain recipes and instructions designed to magically resolve a situation or illness, with some sort of action, a medical potion, and chanting and repeating special phrases, such as Charm No.03 *Against a Dwarf* (fever), No.05 *For Loss of Cattle*, No.07 *For the Water-Elf Disease*, No.08 *For a Swarm of Bees*, No.09 *For Loss of Cattle*, No.10 *For Loss of Cattle*, and No.12 *Against a Wen*.

'The Exeter Book' is a major manuscript of poetry believed to have been produced in the late 10th century, and includes the poems *Pharaoh*, *Alms-Giving*, *The Lord's Prayer I*, *The Partridge*, *Homiletic Fragment II*, and *Wulf and Eadwacer*.

Other Poems include: *A Proverb from Winfrid's Time*, *The Gloria II*, *Bede's Death Song* (*Northumbrian Version*), *Bede's Death Song* (*The Hague Version*), *Bede's Death Song* (*West Saxon Version*), *Latin-English Proverbs*, *The Brussels Cross*, *Caedmon's Hymn* (*Northumbrian Version*), *Caedmon's Hymn* (*West Saxon Version*), *Thureth*, *Aldhelm*, *Durham*, *A Summons to Prayer*, and *Waldere B*.

This book is designed to be of use to anyone studying or with a keen interest in Anglo-Saxon or Old English, clearly showing how the language works, and the beginnings of what would evolve into modern English. This edition is laid out in three columns, the original text, a literal word-for-word translation, a modern translation, and individual word lists for each poem. Also included is an overall word list with over 1,000 definitions.

1 Chronicle Poems

1.1 The Capture of the Five Boroughs

Text

	Ænglisc	Literal	English
1	*Her Eadmund cyning,*	Here Edmund king,	Here King Edmund,
	Engla þeoden,	English lord,	lord of the English,
2	*mæcgea mundbora,*	kinsmen guardian,	Guardian of kinsmen,
	Myrce geeode,	Mercia conquered,	conquered Mercia,
3	*dyre dædfruma,*	dear deed-doer,	The dear doer of deeds,
	swa Dor scadeþ,	as The Dore borders,	as the Dore borders it,
4	*Hwitanwyllesgeat*	Whitwell Gap	The Whitwell Fap
	and Humbra ea,	and Humber river,	and the River Humber,
5	*brada brimstream.*	broad ocean-stream.	broad ocean-stream.
	Burga fife,	Boroughs five,	Five Boroughs,
6	*Ligoraceaster*	Leicester	Leicester
	and Lincylene	and Lincoln	and Lincoln
7	*and Snotingaham,*	and Nottingham,	and Nottingham,
	swylce Stanford eac	likewise Stamford also	also Stamford
8	*and Deoraby.*	and Derby.	and Derby.
	Dæne wæran æror	Danes were before	Danes were previously
9	*under Norðmannum*	under Northmen	under the Northmen
	nyde gebegde	subjected bowed	subjected and bowed
10	*on hæþenra*	in heathen	in heathen
	hæfteclommum	binding-chains	binding chains
11	*lange þrage,*	long for-a-time,	for a long time,
	oþ hie alysde eft	until he released afterwards	until he released them afterwards
12	*for his weorþscipe*	for his worthship	for his worthiness
	wiggendra hleo,	warriors protecting,	protector of warriors,
13	*afera Eadweardes,*	heir-of Eadweard,	son of Eadweard
	Eadmund cyning.	Eadmund king.	King Edmund.

Word List

Ænglisc	English	*Ænglisc*	English
æror	before	*dædfruma*	deed-doer
afera	heir-of	*Dæne*	Danes
alysde	released	*Deoraby*	Derby
and	and	*Dor*	The Dore
brada	broad	*dyre*	dear
brimstream	ocean-stream	*ea*	river
Burga	boroughs	*eac*	also
cyning	king, king	*Eadmund*	Eadmund

6

Ænglisc	English
Eadmund	Edmund
Eadweardes	Edward
eft	afterwards
engla	English
fife	five
for	for
gebegde	bowed
geeode	conquered
hæfteclommum	binding-chains
hæþenra	heathen
her	here
hie	he
his	his
hleo	protecting
Humbra	Humber
Hwitanwyllesgeat	Whitwell Gap
lange	long
Ligoraceaster	Leicester
Lincylene	Lincoln
mæcgea	kinsmen
mundbora	guardian
myrce	Mercia
Norðmannum	Northmen
nyde	subjected
on	in
oþ	until
scadeþ	borders
Snotingaham	Nottingham
Stanford	Stamford
swa	as
swylce	likewise
þeoden	lord
þrage	for-a-time
under	under
wæran	were
weorþscipe	worthship
wiggendra	warriors

1.2 The Coronation of Edgar

Text

Ænglisc	Literal	English

1 Her Eadgar wæs,
  Engla waldend,
	Here Edgar was,
	  English ruler,
		Here Edgar was,
		  ruler of the English,

2 corðre miclum
  to cyninge gehalgod
	assembly great
	  to king consecrated
		in a great assembly
		  consecrated as king

3 on ðære ealdan byrig,
  Acemannesceastre;
	in there old town,
	  Akeman's Town;
		in the old down,
		  Akeman's Town;

4 eac hi igbuend
  oðre worde
	also the islanders
	  another word
		also the islanders
		  by another word

5 beornas Baðan nemnaþ.
  þær wæs blis micel
	children-of-men Bath name.
	  there was rejoicing much
		children of men call it Bath.
		  there was much rejoicing

6 on þam eadgan dæge
  eallum geworden,
	about that blessed day
	  all became,
		about that blessed day
		  come to all,

7 þone niða bearn
  nemnað and cigað
	the conflict children
	  name and call
		those children of conflict
		  name and call it

8 Pentecostenes dæg.
  þær wæs preosta heap,
	Pentecost day.
	  there was priests pile,
		Pentecost day.
		  there was a throng of priests

9 micel muneca ðreat,
  mine gefrege,
	great monk crowd,
	  of mind noted,
		a great crowd of monks
		  of learned minds,

10 gleawra gegaderod.
  And ða agangen wæs
	skilful gathered.
	  And then going was
		and skilful gathered
		  And then had gone

11 tyn hund wintra
  geteled rimes
	ten hundred winters
	  reckoned counted
		ten hundred winters
		  reckoned to be counted

12 fram gebyrdtide
  bremes cyninges,
	from the-birth
	  celebrated king,
		from the birth
		  of the celebrated king,

13 leohta hyrdes,
  buton ðær to lafe þa get
	light keeper,
	  except there to remain then agreed
		keeper of lights,
		  except there remained it was agreed

14 wæs wintergeteles,
  þæs ðe gewritu secgað,
	was winters-numbered,
	  this as writings say,
		there were winters numbered,
		  as the writings say

15 seofon and twentig;
  swa neah wæs sigora frean
	seven and twenty;
	  so nigh was victories lord
		twenty seven;
		  So nigh on had the Lord of Victories

16 ðusend aurnen,
  ða þa ðis gelamp.
	thousand passed,
	  then that this happened.
		a thousand years passed,
		  when this happened.

17 And him Eadmundes
  eafora hæfde
	And he Edmund
	  descendants had
		And his Edmund's
		  descendants had

18 nigon and XX,
  niðweorca heard,
	nine and twenty,
	  conflict bitter,
		twenty nine,
		  in bitter conflict,

19 wintra on worulde,
  ða þis geworden wæs,
	winters in the-world,
	  then it agreed was,
		winters in the world,
		  then it was agreed,

20 and þa on ðam XXX wæs	and then in that thirty was	that then in that thirty years

Ænglisc	Literal	English
ðeoden gehalgod.	the-lord consecrated.	the Lord was consecrated.

Word List

Ænglisc	English	*Ænglisc*	English
acemannesceastre	Akeman's Town	*get*	agreed
agangen	going	*geteled*	reckoned
and	and	*geworden*	agreed
aurnen	passed	*geworden*	became
baðan	Bath	*gewritu*	writings
bearn	children	*gleawra*	skilful
beornas	children-of-men	*hæfde*	had
blis	rejoicing	*heap*	pile
bremes	celebrated	*heard*	bitter
buton	except	*her*	here
byrig	town	*hi*	the
cigað	call	*him*	his
corðre	assembly	*hund*	hundred
cyninge	king	*hyrdes*	keeper
cyninges	king	*igbuend*	islanders
ða	then	*lafe*	remain
dæg	day	*leohta*	light
dæge	day	*micel*	great
ðær	there	*micel*	much
ðære	there	*miclum*	great
ðam	that	*mine*	of mind
ðe	as	*muneca*	monk
ðis	this	*neah*	nigh
ðreat	crowd	*nemnað*	name
ðusend	thousand	*nemnaþ*	name
eac	also	*niða*	murmuring
eadgan	blessed	*niðweorca*	conflict
eadgar	Edgar	*nigon*	nine
eadmundes	Edmund's	*oðre*	another
eafora	descendants	*on*	about
ealdan	old	*on*	in
eallum	all	*pentecostenes*	Pentecost
engla	English	*preosta*	priests
fram	from	*rimes*	counted
frean	lord	*secgað*	say
gebyrdtide	the-birth	*seofon*	seven
gefrege	noted	*sigora*	victories
gegaderod	gathered	*swa*	so
gehalgod	consecrated	*þa*	that
gelamp	happened	*þa*	then

Ænglisc	English
þær	there
þæs	this
þam	that
þeoden	the-lord
þis	it
þone	the
to	to
twentig	twenty
tyn	ten
wæs	was
waldend	ruler
wintergeteles	winters-numbered
wintra	winters
worde	word
worulde	the-world
xx	twenty
xxx	thirty

1.3 The Death of Edward

Text

Ænglisc	Literal	English

1 *Her Eadward kingc,*
    Engla hlaford,
	Here Edward the king,
	    English lord,
		Here Edward the king,
		    lord of the English

2 *sende soþfæste*
    sawle to Criste
	sent righteous
	    soul to Christ
		sent his righteous
		    soul to Christ

3 *on godes wæra,*
    gast haligne.
	in God's keeping,
	    spirit holy.
		in God's keeping,
		    and the holy spirit.

4 *He on worulda her*
    wunode þrage
	He in the world here
	    dwelt for a time
		He in the world here
		    dwelt for a time

5 *on kyneþrymme,*
    cræftig ræda,
	in royal-power,
	    skilful counsel,
		in royal power,
		    with skilful counsel,

6 *XXIIII,*
    freolic wealdend,
	twenty four,
	    freely ruling,
		twenty four,
		    freely ruling,

7 *wintra gerimes,*
    weolan britnode,
	winters number,
	    wealth bestowed,
		winters numbered,
		    bestowed wealth,

8 *and healfe tid,*
    hæleða wealdend,
	and half a time,
	    saviour ruler,
		and half a time
		    saviour ruling,

9 *weold wel geþungen*
    Walum and Scottum
	ruling well gracefully
	    the Welsh and the Scots
		ruled well and gracefully
		    the Welsh and the Scots

10 *and Bryttum eac,*
    byre æðelredes,
	and the Britons too,
	    his child Æthelred's,
		and the Britons too,
		    his child Æthelred's,

11 *Englum and Sexum,*
    oretmægcum,
	The Angles and The Saxons,
	    warriors,
		the Angles and the Saxons,
		    warriors,

12 *swa ymbclyppað*
    cealde brymmas,
	as embraced
	    cold waves,
		as embraced
		    cold waves

13 *þæt eall Eadwarde,*
    æðelum kinge,
	that all Edward,
	    noble king,
		that all Edward,
		    noble king,

14 *hyrdon holdlice*
    hagestealde menn.
	obeyed graciously
	    young and brave men.
		graciously obeyed
		    young and brave men.

15 *Wæs a bliðemod*
    bealuleas kyng,
	Was ever blithe-mood
	    the innocent king,
		Was ever in joyful mood
		    the innocent king,

16 *þeah he lange ær,*
    lande bereafod,
	though he long before,
	    of land bereft,
		though he long before,
		    bereft of land,

17 *wunode wræclastum*
    wide geond eorðan,
	dwelt outcast
	    widely over the earth,
		dwelt as an outcast
		    widely over the earth,

18 *syððan Cnut ofercom*
    kynn æðelredes
	since Canute overcame
	    kin Æthelred's
		since Canute overcame
		    Æthelred's kin

19 *and Dena weoldon*
    deore rice
	and Danes ruled
	    the dear kingdom
		and the Danes ruled
		    the dear kingdom

20 *Engla landes*
    XXVIII
	Engla Land
	    twenty-eight
		England
		    twenty eight

21 *wintra gerimes,*
    welan brytnodon.
	winters numbered,
	    wealth bestowed.
		winters numbered,
		    wealth bestowed.

#	Ænglisc	Translation 1	Translation 2
22	*Syððan forð becom* / *freolice in geatwum*	Since forth came / splendid in trappings	Since forth came / splendid in trappings
23	*kyningc kystum god,* / *clæne and milde,*	a king of virtues good, / chaste and mild,	a king of virtues good, / chaste and mild,
24	*Eadward se æðela,* / *eðel bewerode,*	Edward the noble, / country defended,	Edward the noble, / defended the country,
25	*land and leode,* / *oðþæt lungre becom*	land and people, / until suddenly came	land and people, / until suddenly came
26	*deað se bitera,* / *and swa deore genam*	death so bitter, / and so dear seized	a death so bitter, / and so dear seixed
27	*æþelne of eorðan;* / *englas feredon*	noble of the earth; / angels carried	noble of the earth; / angels carried
28	*soþfæste sawle* / *innan swegles leoht.*	righteous soul / into heaven's light.	his righteous soul / into heaven's light.
29	*And se froda swa þeah* / *befæste þæt rice*	And the wise as nevertheless / entrusted the kingdom	and the wise nevertheless / entrusted the kingdom
30	*heahþungenum menn,* / *Harolde sylfum,*	high-ranking man, / Harold himself,	a high-ranking man, / Harold himself,
31	*æþelum eorle,* / *se in ealle tid*	noble earl, / who in all time	the noble earl, / who in all time
32	*hyrde holdlice* / *hærran sinum*	obeyed loyally / lord his	obeyed loyally / his lord's
33	*wordum and dædum,* / *wihte ne agælde*	words and deeds, / anything not delaying	words and deeds, / not delaying in anything
34	*þæs þe þearf wæs* / *þæs þeodkyninges.*	that the necessary was / this great-king.	that was necessary to / this great king.

Word List

Ænglisc	English	Ænglisc	English
a	ever	*brytnodon*	bestowed
æðela	noble	*bryttum*	the Britons
æðelredes	Æthelred's	*byre*	his child
æðelum	noble	*cealde*	cold
ær	before	*clæne*	chaste
æþelne	noble	*cnut*	Canute
æþelum	noble	*cræftig*	skilful
agælde	delaying	*criste*	Christ
and	and	*dædum*	deeds
bealuleas	the innocent	*deað*	death
becom	came	*dena*	the Danes
befæste	entrusted	*deore*	dear
bereafod	bereft	*deore*	the dear
bewerode	defended	*eac*	too
bitera	bitter	*eadward*	Edward
bliðemod	blithe-mood	*eadwarde*	Edward
britnode	bestowed	*eall*	all
brymmas	waves	*ealle*	all

Ænglisc	English	*Ænglisc*	English
eðel	country	*landes*	Land
engla	Engla	*lange*	long
engla	english	*leode*	people
englas	angels	*leoht*	light
englum	the Angles	*lungre*	suddenly
eorðan	the earth	*menn*	man
eorle	earl	*menn*	men
feredon	carried	*milde*	mild
forð	forth	*ne*	not
freolic	freely	*oðþæt*	until
freolice	splendid	*of*	of
froda	wise	*ofercom*	overcame
gast	spirit	*on*	in
geatwum	trappings	*oretmægcum*	warriors
genam	seized	*ræda*	counsel
geond	over	*rice*	kingdom
gerimes	number	*sawle*	soul
gerimes	numbered	*scottum*	the Scots
geþungen	gracefully	*se*	so
god	good	*se*	the
godes	God's	*se*	who
hæleða	saviour	*sende*	sent
hærran	lord	*sexum*	the Saxons
hagestealde	young and brave	*sinum*	his
haligne	holy	*soþfæste*	righteous
harolde	Harold	*swa*	as
he	he	*swa*	so
heahþungenum	high-ranking	*swegles*	heaven's
healfe	half	*syððan*	since
her	here	*sylfum*	himself
hlaford	lord	*þæs*	that
holdlice	graciously	*þæs*	this
holdlice	loyally	*þæt*	that
hyrde	obeyed	*þæt*	the
hyrdon	obeyed	*þe*	the
in	in	*þeah*	nevertheless
innan	into	*þeah*	though
kingc	the king	*þearf*	necessary
kinge	king	*þeodkyninges*	great-king
kyneþrymme	royal-power	*þrage*	for a time
kyng	king	*tid*	a time
kyningc	a king	*tid*	time
kynn	kin	*to*	to
kystum	of virtues	*wæra*	keeping
land	land	*wæs*	was
lande	of land	*walum*	the Welsh

Ænglisc	English
wealdend	ruler
wel	well
welan	wealth
weolan	wealth
weold	ruling
weoldon	ruled
wide	widely
wihte	anything
wintra	winters
wordum	words
worulda	the world
wræclastum	outcast
wunode	dwelt
xxiiii	twenty four
xxviii	twenty-eight
ymbclyppað	embraced

2 Metrical Charms

2.1 Against a Dwarf

Text

	Ænglisc	Literal	English
1	*Wið dweorh man sceal niman VII lytle oflætan, swylce*	Against a dwarf one shall take seven little wafers, such as	Against a dwarf one must take seven little wafers, such as
2	*man mid ofrað, and writan þas naman on ælcre oflætan:*	one with offertory, and write these names on each wafer:	the one makes offertory with, and write these names on each wafer:
3	*Maximianus, Malchus, Iohannes, Martimianus, Dionisius*	Maximianus, Malchus, Iohannes, Martimianus, Dionisius	Maximianus, Malchus, Iohannes, Martimianus, Dionisius,
4	*Constantinus, Serafion. þænne eft þæt galdor, þæt*	Constantinus, Serafion. Then after that chant, that	Constantinus, Serafion. Then after that chant, that
5	*her æfter cweð, man sceal singan, ærest on þæt wynstre*	here after say, one shall sing, first in the left	which is here after said, one shall sing, first in the left
6	*eare, þænne on þæt swiðre eare, þænne bufan þæs mannes*	ear, then in the right ear, then above the person's	ear, then in the right ear, then above the person's
7	*moldan. And ga þænne an mædenman to and ho hit on*	top-of-the-head. And let then a maiden go to and hang it about	top of the head. And then let a maiden go to them and hang it about
8	*his sweoran, and do man swa þry dagas; him bið sona sel.*	his neck, and do one so three days; to-him be soon better.	his neck, and do so for three days, he will soon be better.
9	*Her com in gangan, inswiden wiht,*	Here came in walking, singed creature,	Here came in walking, a singed creature,
10	*hæfde him his haman on handa, cwæð þæt þu his hæncgest wære,*	had he his horse-collar in hand, saying that you his horse were,	he had his horse collar in hand, saying that you were his horse,
11	*legde þe his teage an sweoran. Ongunnan him of þæm lande liþan;*	laid then his ties on neck. Began he of that land journey;	he then laid his ties on your neck. He began a land journey;
12	*sona swa hy of þæm lande coman, þa ongunnan him ða liþu colian.*	as soon as they of that land came, then began he the limbs became-cold.	as soon as they came from the land, then the limbs began to cool.
13	*þa com in gangan dweores sweostar;*	Then came in walking the dwarf's sister;	Then came walking in the dwarf's sister;
14	*þa geændade heo and aðas swor*	then interceded she and oaths swore	then she interceded and swore oaths
15	*ðæt næfre þis ðæm adlegan derian ne moste,*	that never this the sick-person harm not be able to,	that this beast may never the sick person be able to harm,
16	*ne þæm þe þis galdor begytan mihte,*	nor they that this chant obtain might,	nor the one who this chant might obtain,

17   *oððe þe þis galdor*   or that this chant   or that this chant
       ongalan cuþe.   recite be able to.   is able to recite.
18   *Amen. Fiað.*   Amen. Let it be so.   Amen. Let it be so.

Word List

Ænglisc	English	Ænglisc	English
aðas	oaths	*handa*	hand
adlegan	sick-person	*heo*	she
æfter	after	*her*	here
ælcre	each	*him*	he
ærest	first	*him*	to-him
amen	amen	*his*	his
an	a	*hit*	it
an	on	*ho*	hang
and	and	*hy*	they
begytan	obtain	*in*	in
bið	be	*inswiden*	singed
bufan	above	*iohannes*	Iohannes
colian	became-cold	*lande*	land
com	came	*legde*	laid
coman	came	*liþan*	journey
constantinus	Constantinus	*liþu*	limbs
cuþe	be able to	*lytle*	little
cwæð	saying	*mædenman*	maiden
cweð	say	*malchus*	Malchus
ða	the	*man*	one
ðæm	the	*mannes*	person's
ðæt	that	*martimianus*	Martimianus
dagas	days	*maximianus*	Maximianus
derian	harm	*mid*	with
dionisius	Dionisius	*mihte*	might
do	do	*moldan*	top-of-the-head
dweores	the dwarf's	*moste*	be able to
dweorh	a dwarf	*næfre*	never
eare	ear	*naman*	names
eft	after	*ne*	nor
fiað	let it be so	*ne*	not
ga	let	*niman*	take
galdor	chant	*oððe*	or
gangan	walking	*of*	of
geændade	interceded	*oflætan*	wafer
hæfde	had	*oflætan*	wafers
hæncgest	horse	*ofrað*	offertory
haman	horse-collar	*on*	about

Ænglisc	English
on	in
on	on
ongalan	recite
ongunnan	began
sceal	shall
sel	better
serafion	Serafion
singan	sing
sona	as soon
sona	soon
swa	as
swa	so
sweoran	neck
sweostar	sister
swiðre	right
swor	swore
swylce	such as
teage	ties
þa	then
þæm	that
þæm	they
þænne	then
þæs	the
þæt	that
þæt	the
þas	these
þe	that
þe	then
þis	this
þry	three
þu	you
to	go to
vii	seven
wære	were
wið	against
wiht	creature
writan	write
wynstre	left

2.2   For Loss of Cattle

Text

	Ænglisc	Literal	English
1	*þonne þe mon ærest secge þæt þin ceap sy losod, þonne*	then that someone first says that your property is lost, then	When someone first says that your property is lost, then
2	*cweð þu ærest, ær þu elles hwæt cweþe:*	say you first, before you anything-else hear say:	you say first, before you say anything else:
3	*Bæðleem hatte seo buruh þe Crist on acænned wæs,*	Bethlehem named the town that Christ in brought-forth was,	The town is called Bethlehem where Christ was born,
4	*seo is gemærsod geond ealne middangeard;*	it is made-famous around all middle-earth;	and it is famous around all the earth;
5	*swa þyos dæd for monnum mære gewurþe*	so this deed before men distinguished become	so this deed for mankind became distinguished
6	*þurh þa haligan Cristes rode! Amen. Gebide þe þonne*	through the holy Christ's cross! Amen. Abide then from-there	through the holy Christ's cross! Amen. Look then from there
7	*þriwa east and cweþ þonne þriwa: Crux Christi ab oriente*	three-times east and say then three-times: The cross of Christ from the east	three times east and then say three times: The cross of Christ from the east
8	*reducað. Gebide þe þonne þriwa west and cweð þonne*	is led. Abide then there three-times west and say there	is led. Look then there three times west and say there
9	*þriwa: Crux Christi ab occidente reducat. Gebide þe*	three-times: The cross of Christ from the west is led. Abide then	three times: The cross of Christ from the west is led. Look then
10	*þonne þriwa suð and cweþ þriwa: Crux Christi ab austro*	from there three-times south and say three-times: The cross of Christ from the south	from there three times south and say three times: The cross of Christ from the south
11	*reducat. Gebide þonne þriwa norð and cweð þriwa: Crux*	is led. Abide then three-times north and say three-times: The cross	is led. Look then three times north and say three times: The cross
12	*Christi ab aquilone reducað, crux Christi abscondita est et*	of Christ from the north is led, the cross of Christ hidden is and	of Christ from the north is led, the cross of Christ is hidden and
13	*inuenta est. Iudeas Crist ahengon, dydon dæda þa*	found is. Judas Christ hung up, doing deeds the	is found. Judas hung up Christ, doing the deeds
14	*wyrrestan, hælon þæt hy forhelan ne mihtan. Swa þeos*	worst, covering that he hidden not might. So this	the worst, covering so that he could not be hidden. So this
15	*dæd nænige þinga forholen ne wurþe þurh þa haligan*	deed none thing hidden not become through the holy	deed nothing may become hidden through the holy
16	*Cristes rode. Amen.*	Christ's cross. Amen.	Christ's cross. Amen.

Word List

Ænglisc	English	*Ænglisc*	English
ab	from (Latin)	ær	before
abscondita	hidden (Latin)	ærest	first
acænned	brought-forth	ahengon	hung up

Ænglisc	English	*Ænglisc*	English
amen	amen	occidente	the west (Latin)
and	and	on	in
aquilone	the north (Latin)	oriente	the east (Latin)
austro	the south (Latin)	reducað	is led (Latin)
bæðleem	Bethlehem	reducat	is led (Latin)
buruh	town	rode	cross
ceap	property	secge	says
christi	of Christ	seo	it
crist	Christ	seo	the
cristes	Christ's	suð	south
crux	the cross (Latin)	swa	so
cweð	say	sy	is
cweþ	say	þa	the
cweþe	say	þæt	that
dæd	deed	þe	that
dæda	deeds	þe	then
dydon	doing	þeos	this
ealne	all	þin	your
east	east	þinga	thing
elles	anything-else	þonne	from there
est	is (Latin)	þonne	from-there
et	and (Latin)	þonne	then
for	for	þonne	there
forhelan	hidden	þriwa	three-times
forholen	hidden	þu	you
gebide	abide	þurh	through
gemærsod	made-famous	þyos	this
geond	around	wæs	was
gewurþe	become	west	west
hælon	covering	wurþe	become
haligan	holy	wyrrestan	worst
hatte	named		
hwæt	hear		
hy	he		
inuenta	found (Latin)		
is	is		
iudeas	Judas		
losod	lost		
mære	distinguished		
middangeard	middle-earth		
mihtan	might		
mon	someone		
monnum	mankind		
nænige	none		
ne	not		
norð	north		

2.3 For the Water-Elf Disease

Text

	Ænglisc	Literal	English
1	*Gif mon biþ on wæterælfadle, þonne beoþ him þa hand-*	If one be in water elf disease, whereby be his being hand-	If one has water elf disease, where his hand
2	*næglas wonne and þa eagan tearige and wile locian niþer.*	nails dark and being eyes teary and willing to look downwards.	nails are dark and his eyes are teary and willing to look downwards.
3	*Do him þis to læcedome: eoforþrote, cassuc, fone nioþo-*	Do him this to remedy: carline thistle, cassock, take from below-	Do him this remedy: carline thistle, cassock, take from below
4	*weard, eowberge, elehtre, eolone, merscmealwan crop,*	keep, yew berry, lupine, elecampane, marshmallow sprout,	keep, yew berry, lupine, elecampane, marshmallow sprout,
5	*fenminte, dile, lilie, attorlaþe, polleie, marubie, docce, ellen,*	fen mint, dill, lily, cock's spur grass, pennyroyal, marrabulum, sorrel, elder,	fen mint, dill, ily, cock's spur grass, pennyroyal, marrabulum, sorrel, elder,
6	*felterre, wermod, streawbergean leaf, consolde; ofgeot mid*	felterry, wormwood, strawberry leaf, comfrey; soak with	felterry, wormwood, strawberry leaf, comfrey; soak with
7	*ealaþ, do hæligwæter to, sing þis gealdor ofer þriwa:*	ale, do holy water to, sing this chant over three times:	ale, add holy water to, and sing this chant over it three times:
8	*Ic benne awrat betest beadowræda,*	I this wound wrote the best battle bandage,	I have written for this wound the best battle bandage,
9	*swa benne ne burnon, ne burston,*	so the wound does not burn, nor burst,	so the wound does not burn, nor burst,
10	*ne fundian, ne feologan,*	neither forwards, nor become fallow,	neither forwards, nor becoming fallow,
11	*ne hoppettan, ne wund waxsian,*	neither throb, nor wound geow,	neither throb, nor wound grow,
12	*ne dolh diopian; ac him self healde halewæge,*	nor the pain deepen; but he himself hold the hallows,	nor the pain deepen; but he himself holds the hallows,
13	*ne ace þe þon ma, þe eorþan on eare ace.*	nor grow though from there greater, though the earth in ears grows.	nor grow though from there any greater, though the earth in ears grows.
14	*Sing þis manegum siþum: Eorþe þe onbere eallum hire*	Sing this many afterwards: Earth though withers all these	Sing this many times afterwards: 'Though the earth withers, all these
15	*mihtum and mægenum. þas galdor mon mæg singan on*	might and power. this chant one may sing over	might and power'. This chant one may sing over
16	*wunde.*	wounds.	the wounds.

Word List

Ænglisc	English	*Ænglisc*	English
ac	but	*healde*	hold
ace	grow	*him*	he
ace	grows	*him*	him
and	and	*him*	his
attorlaþe	cock's spur grass	*hire*	these
awrat	wrote	*hoppettan*	throb
beadowræda	battle bandage	*ic*	I
benne	the wound	*læcedome*	remedy
benne	this wound	*leaf*	leaf
beoþ	be	*lilie*	lily
betest	the best	*locian*	to look
biþ	be	*ma*	greater
burnon	burn	*mæg*	may
burston	burst	*mægenum*	power
cassuc	cassock	*manegum*	many
consolde	comfrey	*marubie*	marrabulum
crop	sprout	*merscmealwan*	marshmallow
dile	dill	*mid*	with
diopian	deepen	*mihtum*	might
do	do	*mon*	one
docce	sorrel	*næglas*	nails
dolh	the pain	*ne*	does not
eagan	eyes	*ne*	neither
ealaþ	ale	*ne*	nor
eallum	all	*nioþo*	from below
eare	ears	*niþer*	downwards
elehtre	lupine	*ofer*	over
ellen	elder	*ofgeot*	soak
eoforþrote	carline thistle	*on*	in
eolone	elecampane	*on*	over
eorþan	the earth	*onbere*	withers
eorþe	earth	*polleie*	pennyroyal
eowberge	yew berry	*self*	himself
felterre	felterry	*sing*	sing
fenminte	fen mint	*singan*	sing
feologan	become fallow	*siþum*	afterwards
fone	take	*streawbergean*	strawberry
fundian	forwards	*swa*	so
galdor	chant	*tearige*	teary
gealdor	chant	*þa*	being
gif	if	*þas*	this
hæligwæter	holy water	*þe*	though
halewæge	the hallows	*þis*	this
hand	hand	*þon*	from there

Ænglisc	English
þonne	whereby
þriwa	three times
to	to
wæterælfadle	water elf disease
waxsian	grow
weard	keep
wermod	wormwood
wile	willing
wonne	dark
wund	wound
wunde	wounds

2.4   For a Swarm of Bees

Text

Ænglisc	Literal	English
1 *Wið ymbe nim eorþan,*	Against a swarm of bees take	Against a swarm of bees take
oferweorp mid þinre swiþran	earth, throw down with your right	some earth, throwing down with your right
2 *handa under þinum swiþran fet, and cwet:*	hand under your right foot, and saying:	hand under your right foot, and saying:
3 *"Fo ic under fot,*	"Take I under foot,	"I take this under foot,
funde ic hit.	found I it.	I found it.
4 *Hwæt, eorðe mæg*	Hear, earth may be	Hear, earth may be
wið ealra wihta gehwilce	against all beings every	against each and every being
5 *and wið andan*	and against injury	and against injury
and wið æminde	and against forgetfulness	and against forgetfulness
6 *and wið þa micelan".*	and against the great".	and against the great".
7 *And wiððon forweorp ofer greot, þonne hi swirman, and cweð:*	And afterwards throw over earth, those the swarming, and say:	And afterwards throw earth over those swarming and say:
8 *"Sitte ge, sigewif,*	"Sit you, victorious-women,	"Sit you, victorious women,
sigað to eorþan!	sink to the earth!	sink ot the earth!
9 *Næfre ge wilde*	Never you wild	Never will you wildly
to wuda fleogan.	to the woods fly.	fly to the woods.
10 *Beo ge swa gemindige*	Be you as mindful	Be as mindful
mines godes,	my wellbeing,	of my wellbeing
11 *swa bið manna gehwilc*	as be men each	as each man is
metes and eþeles.	food and homeland".	to his food and homeland".

Word List

Ænglisc	English	Ænglisc	English
æminde	forgetfulness	*forweorp*	throw
and	and	*fot*	foot
andan	injury	*funde*	found
beo	be	*ge*	you
bið	be	*gehwilc*	each
cweð	say	*gehwilce*	every
cwet	saying	*gemindige*	mindful
ealra	all	*godes*	wellbeing
eorðe	earth	*greot*	earth
eorþan	earth	*handa*	hand
eorþan	the earth	*hi*	the
eþeles	homeland	*hit*	it
fet	foot	*hwæt*	hear
fleogan	fly	*ic*	I
fo	take	*mæg*	may be

Ænglisc	English
manna	men
mannes	man's
metes	food
micelan	great
mid	with
mines	my
næfre	never
nim	take
ofer	over
oferweorp	throw down
sigað	sink
sigewif	victorious-women
sitte	sit
swa	as
swirman	swarming
swiþran	right
þa	the
þinre	your
þinum	your
þonne	those
to	to
tungan	tongue
under	under
wið	against
wiððon	afterwards
wihta	beings
wilde	wild
wuda	the woods
ymbe	a swarm of bees

2.5　For Loss of Cattle

Text

	Ænglisc	Literal	English
1	*Ne forstolen ne forholen nanuht, þæs ðe ic age, þe ma ðe*	Not stolen not hidden nothing, of-that which I own, any more which	May nothing be stolen or hidden which I own, any more than
2	*mihte Herod urne drihten. Ic geþohte sancte Eadelenan*	might Herod our Lord. I thought Saint Blessed-Helen	Herod might our Lord. I thought of the blessed Saint Helen
3	*and ic geþohte Crist on rode ahangen; swa ic þence þis feoh*	and I thought Christ on cross hanged; thus I think this cattle	and I thought of Christ hanged on the cross; thus I think to this cattle
4	*to findanne, næs to oðfeorrganne, and to witanne, næs to*	to find, by-no-means to drive-away, and to protect, by-no-means to	to find, not to drive away, and to protect, not to
5	*oðwyrceanne, and to lufianne, næs to oðlædanne.*	destroy, and to love, by-no-means to lead-off.	destroy, to love, not to lead away.
6	*Garmund,* 　　*godes ðegen,*	Garmund, 　　God's thane,	Garmund, 　　God's servant,
7	*find þæt feoh* 　　*and fere þæt feoh*	find that cattle 　　and drive that cattle	find that cattle 　　and drive that cattle
8	*and hafa þæt feoh* 　　*and heald þæt feoh*	and have that cattle 　　and hold that cattle	and have that cattle 　　and hold that cattle
9	*and fere ham þæt feoh.*	and drive home that cattle.	and drive home that cattle.
10	*þæt he næfre næbbe landes,* 　　*þæt he hit oðlæde,*	that he never not-have land, 　　that he it lead-off,	so that he may not have land, 　　that he may lead it away,
11	*ne foldan,* 　　*þæt hit oðferie,*	not earth, 　　that he drive-off,	nor earth, 　　that he may drive it away,
12	*ne husa,* 　　*þæt he hit oðhealde.*	not houses, 　　that he it keep-away.	nor any houses, 　　that he may keep it away.
13	*Gif hyt hwa gedo,* 　　*ne gedige hit him næfre!*	If it who do, 　　not prosper it him never!	If anyone would do this, 　　may they never prosper from it!
14	*Binnan þrym nihtum* 　　*cunne ic his mihta,*	Within three nights 　　know I his might,	Within three nights 　　I will know his powers,
15	*his mægen and his mihta* 　　*and his mundcræftas.*	his strengths and his powers 　　and his protection-powers.	his strenghts and his powers 　　and his powers of protection.
16	*Eall he weornige,* 　　*swa syre wudu weornie,*	All he waste-away, 　　as rotten wood waste-away,	May he all waste away, 　　as rotten wood waste away,
17	*swa breðel seo swa þystel,*	as brittle be as thistle,	be as brittle as a thistle,
18	*se ðe ðis feoh* 　　*oðfergean þence*	he who this cattle 　　drive-away intend	he who this cattle 　　might intend to drive away
19	*oðđe ðis orf* 　　*oðehtian ðence.*	or this cattle 　　disposess intent.	or this cattle 　　might have intent to disposess.

20 *Amen.* Amen. Amen.

Word List

Ænglisc	English	*Ænglisc*	English
age	own	*landes*	land
ahangen	hanged	*lufianne*	love
amen	amen	*ma*	more
and	and	*mægen*	strengths
binnan	within	*mihta*	might
breðel	brittle	*mihta*	powers
crist	Christ (a name)	*mihte*	might
cunne	know	*mundcræftas*	protection-powers
ðe	which	*næbbe*	not-have
ðe	who	*næfre*	never
ðegen	thane	*næs*	by-no-means
ðence	intent	*nanuht*	nothing
ðis	this	*ne*	not
drihten	lord	*nihtum*	nights
eadelenan	Blessed-Helen (a name)	*oððe*	or
		oðehtian	disposess
eall	all	*oðfeorrganne*	drive-away
feoh	cattle	*oðfergean*	drive-away
fere	drive	*oðferie*	drive-off
find	find	*oðhealde*	keep-away
findanne	find	*oðlædanne*	lead-off
foldan	earth	*oðlæde*	lead-off
forholen	hidden	*oðwyrceanne*	destroy
forstolen	stolen	*on*	on
garmund	Garmund (a name)	*orf*	cattle
gedige	prosper	*rode*	cross
gedo	do	*sancte*	saint
geþohte	thought	*se*	he
gif	if	*seo*	be
godes	God's	*swa*	as
hafa	have	*swa*	thus
ham	home	*syre*	rotten
he	he	*þæs*	of-that
heald	hold	*þæt*	that
herod	Herod (a name)	*þe*	any
him	him	*þence*	intend
his	his	*þence*	think
hit	he	*þis*	this
hit	it	*þrym*	three
husa	houses	*þystel*	thistle
hwa	who	*to*	to
hyt	it	*urne*	our
ic	I		

Ænglisc	English
weornie	waste-away
weornige	waste-away
witanne	protect
wudu	wood

2.6 For Loss of Cattle

Text

	Ænglisc	Literal	English
1	*ðis man sceal cweðan ðonne his ceapa hwilcne man for-*	this a man shall speak when his cattle which man because-	This a man shall speak when for when his cattle
2	*stolenne. Cwyð ær he ænyg oþer word cweðe:*	stolen. Say before he any other word say:	is stolen. He shall say this before any other word:
3	*Bethlem hattæ seo burh*	Bethlehem is named the town	There is a town called Bethlehem
	ðe Crist on geboren wes,	that Christ in born was,	that Christ was born in,
4	*seo is gemærsod*	it is made famous	it is made famous
	ofer ealne middangeard;	over all middle-earth;	over all of middle-earth;
5	*swa ðeos dæd wyrþe*	so this deed worthy	so this deed becomes
	for monnum mære,	for mankind glorious,	famous for all mankind,
6	*per crucem Christi! And gebide þe ðonne þriwa east and*	by the cross of Christ! And look it then three-times east and	by the cross of Christ!' And let him look three times to the east and
7	*cweð þriwa: Crux Christi ab oriente reducat. And III*	say three-times: The cross of Christ from the east led. And three-times	say three times: 'The cross of Christ was led from the east'. And three times
8	*west and cweð: Crux Christi ab occidente reducat. And*	west and say: The cross of Christ from the west led. And	west and say: 'The cross of Christ was led from the west'. And
9	*III suð and cweð: Crux Christi a meridie reducant. And*	three-times south and say: The cross of Christ from the south led. And	three times south and say: 'The cross of Christ was led from the south'. And
10	*III norð and cweð: Crux Christi abscondita sunt et inuenta*	three-times north and say: The cross of Christ was hidden they and found	three times north and say: 'The cross of Christ was hidden by them and found
11	*est. Iudeas Crist ahengon, gedidon him dæda þa wyrstan;*	is. Judas Christ hung up, did he deeds the worst;	it is'. Judas hung up Christ, and he did the worst deeds;
12	*hælon þæt hi forhelan ne mihton. Swa næfre ðeos dæd*	it that it conceal not might. So never this deed	that it could not be concealed. So never this deed
13	*forholen ne wyrðe per crucem Christi.*	hidden not become by the cross of Christ.	can become hidden by the cross of Christ

Word List

Ænglisc	English	*Ænglisc*	English
a	from	*Bethlem*	Bethlehem
ab	from	*burh*	town
abscondita	was hidden	*ceapa*	cattle
ænyg	any	*Christi*	of Christ
ær	before	*Crist*	Christ
ahengon	hung up	*crucem*	the cross
And	and	*Crux*	the cross
and	and	*cweð*	say

Ænglisc	English	*Ænglisc*	English
cweðan	speak	*oriente*	the east
cweðe	say	*oþer*	other
Cwyð	say	*per*	by
dæd	deed	*reducant*	led
dæda	deeds	*reducat*	led
ðe	that	*sceal*	shall
ðeos	this	*seo*	it
ðis	this	*seo*	the
ðonne	then	*stolenne*	stolen
ðonne	when	*suð*	south
ealne	all	*sunt*	they
east	east	*swa*	so
est	is	*þa*	the
et	and	*þæt*	that
for	because	*þe*	it
for	for	*þriwa*	three-times
forhelan	conceal	*wes*	was
forholen	hidden	*west*	west
gebide	look	*word*	word
geboren	born	*wyrðe*	become
gedidon	did	*wyrstan*	worst
gemærsod	made famous	*wyrþe*	become
hælon	hit		
hattæ	is named		
he	he		
hi	it		
him	he		
his	his		
hwilcne	which		
III	three-times		
inuenta	found		
is	is		
Iudeas	Judas		
mære	famous		
man	a man		
man	man		
meridie	the south		
middangeard	middle-earth		
mihton	might		
monnum	mankind		
næfre	never		
ne	not		
norð	north		
occidente	the west		
ofer	over		
on	in		

2.7 Against a Wen

Text

	Ænglisc	Literal	English

1	*Wenne, wenne,*
	    wenchichenne,
		Wen, wen,
		    little wen,
			Wen, wen,
			    little wen,

2	*her ne scealt þu timbrien,*
	    ne nenne tun habben,
		here not shall you build,
		    nor any dwelling have,
			you shall not build here,
			    nor have any dwelling,

3	*ac þu scealt north eonene*
	    to þan nihgan berhge,
		but you shall north pass
		    to the next hill,
			but you shall pass north
			    to the next hill,

4	*þer þu hauest, ermig,*
	    enne broþer.
		there you have, in pain,
		    a brother.
			there you have, in pain,
			    a brother.

5	*He þe sceal legge*
	    leaf et heafde.
		He then shall lay
		    a leaf on face.
			He shall then lay
			    a leaf upon your face.

6	*Under fot wolues,*
	    under ueþer earnes,
		Under foot the wolf's,
		    under wing the eagle's,
			Under the wolf's foot,
			    under the eagle's wing,

7	*under earnes clea,*
	    a þu geweornie.
		under eagle's claw,
		    all you wither away.
			under the eagle's claw,
			    and you shall all wither away.

8	*Clinge þu*
	    alswa col on heorþe,
		Shrink you
		    as coal on hearth,
			You will shrink
			    as coal on a hearth,

9	*scring þu*
	    alswa scerne awage,
		shrivel you
		    as dung away,
			you will shrivel
			    as dung away,

10	*and weorne*
	    alswa weter on anbre.
		and evaporate
		    as water in bucket.
			and evapourate
			    as water in a bucket.

11	*Swa litel þu gewurþe*
	    alswa linsetcorn,
		As little you become
		    as linseed,
			You will become as little
			    as linseed,

12	*and miccli lesse*
	    alswa anes handwurmes hupeban,
		and much smaller
		    as a hand-worm's hipbone,
			and much smaller
			    as a hand-worm's hip bone,

13	*and alswa litel þu gewurþe*
	    þet þu nawiht gewurþe.
		and as little you become
		    that you nothing become.
			and become so little
			    that you shall become nothing.

Word List

Ænglisc	English		
a	all	*clinge*	shrink
ac	but	*col*	coal
alswa	as	*earnes*	the eagle's
anbre	bucket	*earnes*	eagle's
and	and	*enne*	a
anes	a	*eonene*	pass
awage	away	*ermig*	in pain
berhge	hill	*et*	on
broþer	brother	*fot*	foot
clea	claw	*geweornie*	wither away
		gewurþe	become

habben	have
handwurmes	hand-worm's
hauest	have
he	he
heafde	face
heorþe	hearth
her	here
hupeban	hipbone
leaf	a leaf
legge	lay
lesse	smaller
linsetcorn	linseed
litel	little
miccli	much
nawiht	nothing
ne	not
ne	nor
nenne	any
nihgan	next
north	north
on	on
on	in
sceal	shall
scealt	shall
scerne	dung
scring	shrivel
swa	as
þan	the
þe	then
þer	there
þet	that
þu	you
timbrien	build
to	to
tun	dwelling
ueþer	wing
under	under
wenchichenne	little wen
wenne	wen
weorne	evaporate
weter	water
wolues	the wolf's

3 Other Poems

3.1 A Proverb from Winfrid's Time

Text

Ænglisc	Literal	English
1 Oft daed lata 　　domę foręldit,	Often deed slack 　　delay glory,	Often the slack of deed 　　delay seeking glory,
2 sigisiþa gahwem, 　　swyltit þi ana.	victorious undertaking, 　　die therefore alone.	in each victorious undertaking, 　　and die therefore alone.

Word List

Ænglisc	English
ana	alone
daed	deed
domę	glory
forędit	delays
gahwem	undertaking
lata	slack
oft	often
sigisiþa	successful
swyltit	dies
þi	therefore

3.2 The Gloria II

Text

Ænglisc	Literal	English
1 Wuldor sy ðe and wurðmynt, wereda drihten,	Glory be to-thee and honour, army lord,	Glory be to thee and honour, lord of armies,
2 fæder on foldan, fægere gemæne,	father on earth, good universal,	father on earth, the universal good,
3 mid sylfan sunu and soðum gaste.	with his-self son and true spirit.	with his own son and the true spirit.
4 Amen.	Amen.	Amen.

Word List

Ænglisc	English
amen	amen
and	and
ðe	to-thee
drihten	lord
fæder	father
fægere	good
foldan	earth
gaste	spirit
gemæne	universal
mid	with
on	on
soðum	true
sunu	son
sy	be
sylfan	his-self
wereda	army
wuldor	glory
wurðmynt	honour

3.3 Bede's Death Song (Northumbrian Version)

Text

	Ænglisc	Literal	English
1	Fore þaem neidfaerae	For the needed-journey	For the necessary journey
	naenig wiurðit	none will-be	no one will be
2	þoncsnotturra,	thought-wiser,	wiser in thought
	þan him þarf sie	than he needs to-be	than he needs to be
3	to ymbhycggannae	to about-think	to consider
	aer his hiniongae	before he from-here-goes	before he goes from here
4	huaet his gastae	what-of his spirit	what of his spirit
	godaes aeðða yflaes	good or evil	is good or evil
5	aefter deoðdaege	after death-day	after his death day
	doemid weorðae.	deemed of-worth.	will be judged of its worth.

Word List

Ænglisc	English
aeðða	or
aefter	after
aer	before
deoðdaege	death-day
doemid	deemed
fore	for
gastae	spirit
godaes	good
him	he
hiniongae	from-here-goes
his	he
his	his
huaet	what-of
naenig	none
neidfaerae	needed-journey
sie	to-be
þaem	the
þan	than
þarf	needs
þoncsnotturra	thought-wiser
to	to
weorðae	of-worth
wiurðit	will-be
yflaes	evil
ymbhycggannae	about-think

3.4 Bede's Death Song (The Hague Version)

Text

Ænglisc	Literal	English
1 *Fore ðaem nedfere*	For the needed-journey	For the necessary journey
nenig wiorðeð	none will-be	no one will be
2 *ðonosnottorra*	thought-wiser	wiser in thought
ðon him ðearf siae	than he needs to-be	than he needs to be
3 *to ymbhycgenne*	to about-think	to consider
aer his hinionge	before he from-here-goes	before he goes from here
4 *hwet his gastæ*	what-of his spirit	what of his spirit
godes oððe yfles	good or evil	is good or evil
5 *efter deaðdege*	after death-day	after his death day
doemed wiorðe.	deemed of-worth.	will be judged of its worth.

Word List

Ænglisc	English
aer	before
ðaem	the
deaðdege	death-day
ðearf	needs
doemed	deemed
ðon	than
ðonosnottorra	thought-wiser
efter	after
fore	for
gastæ	spirit
godes	good
him	he
hinionge	from-here-goes
his	he
his	his
hwet	what-of
nedfere	needed-journey
nenig	none
oððe	or
siae	to-be
to	to
wiorðe.	of-worth
wiorðeð	will-be
yfles	evil
ymbhycgenne	about-think

3.5 Bede's Death Song (The West Saxon Version)

Text

	Ænglisc	Literal	English
1	*For þam nedfere*	For the needed-journey	For the necessary journey
	næni wyrþeþ	none will-be	no one will be
2	*þances snotera,*	thought wiser,	wiser in thought
	þonne him þearf sy	than he needs to-be	than he needs to be
3	*to gehicgenne*	to think	to consider
	ær his heonengange	before he from-here-goes	before he goes from here
4	*hwæt his gaste*	what-of his spirit	what of his spirit
	godes oþþe yfeles	good or evil	is good or evil
5	*æfter deaþe heonon*	after death from-here	after his death day
	demed weorþe.	deemed of-worth.	will be judged of its worth.

Word List

Ænglisc	English
æfter	after
ær	before
deaþe	death
demed	deemed
for	for
gaste	spirit
gehicgenne	think
godes	good
heonengange	from-here-goes
heonon	from-here
him	he
his	he
his	his
hwæt	what-of
næni	none
nedfere	needed-journey
oþþe	or
snotera	wiser
sy	to-be
þam	the
þances	thought
þearf	needs
þonne	than
to	to
weorþe	of-worth
wyrþeþ	will-be
yfeles	evil

3.6 The Brussels Cross

Text

Ænglisc	Literal	English

1   *Rod is min nama.*
    Geo ic ricne cyning
2   *bær byfigynde,*
    blode bestemed.
3   *þas rode het æþlmær wyrican*

    and Aðelwold hys beroþor
4   *Criste to lofe for ælfrices*
    saule hyra beroþor.

Cross is my name.
    Once I a-powerful king
bore trembling,
    bloodied wet.
This cross commanded Æthelmaer made
    and Æthelwold his brother
Christ for love because-of
    Ælfric's soul their brother.

Cross is my name.
    Once, a powerful king I
bore trembling,
    bloodied wet.
this cross Æthelmaer commanded made
    and Æthelwold his brother
for the love of Christ and for
    Ælfric's soul, their brother.

Word List

Ænglisc	English
Aðelwold	Æthelwold (a name)
Ælfrices	Ælfric's (a name)
Æþlmær	Æthelmaer (a name)
and	and
bær	bore
beroþor	brother
bestemed	wet
blode	bloodied
byfigynde	trembling
Criste	Christ (a name)
cyning	king
for	because-of
Geo	once
het	commanded
hyra	their
hys	his
ic	I
is	is
lofe	love
min	my
nama	name
ricne	a-powerful
Rod	cross
rode	cross
saule	soul
þas	this
to	for
wyrican	made

3.7 Latin-English Proverbs

Text

Ænglisc	Literal	English

1 *Ardor frigesscit,*
  nitor squalescit,
	Heat grows-cold,
	  shining grows-dirty,
		Heat grows cold,
		  that which shines grows dirty,

2 *amor abolescit,*
  lux obtenebrescit.
	love fades-away,
	  light grows-dark.
		love fades away,
		  light grows dark.

3 *Hat acolað,*
  hwit asolað,
	Heat grows-cold,
	  white grows-dirty,
		Heat grows cold,
		  that which is white grows dirty,

4 *leof alaðaþ,*
 	
  leoht aðystrað.
	love becomes-loathed,
	
	  light grows-dark.
		that which is loved becomes loathed,
		  light grows dark

5 *Senescunt omnia*
  que æterna non sunt.
	Grows-old everything
	  which eternal not they-are.
		Everything grows old
		  of which they are not eternal.

6 *æghwæt forealdað*
  þæs þe ece ne byð.
	Everything grows-old
	  that which eternal not be.
		Everything grows old
		  that is not eternal.

Word List

Ænglisc	English	*Ænglisc*	English
abolescit	fades-away (Latin)	*que*	which (Latin)
acolað	grows-cold	*senescunt*	grows-old (Latin)
aðystrað	grows-dark	*squalescit*	grows-dirty (Latin)
æghwæt	everything	*sunt*	they-are (Latin)
æterna	eternal (Latin)	*þæs*	that
alaðaþ	becomes-loathed	*þe*	which
amor	love (Latin)		
ardor	heat (Latin)		
asolað	grows-dirty		
byð	be		
ece	eternal		
forealdað	grows-old		
frigesscit	grows-cold (Latin)		
hat	heat		
hwit	white		
leof	love		
leoht	light		
lux	light (Latin)		
ne	not		
nitor	shining (Latin)		
non	not (Latin)		
obtenebrescit	grows-dark (Latin)		
omnia	everything (Latin)		

3.8 Caedmon's Hymn (Northumbrian Version)

Text

	Ænglisc	Literal	English

1	Nu scylun hergan
	    hefaenricaes uard,
		Now shall-we honour
		    heaven-kingdom's ward,
			Now shall we honour
			    the guardian of heaven,

2	metudæs maecti
	    end his modgidanc,
		the-measurer's might
		    and his mind-plans,
			the meaurer's might
			    and his mind's design,

3	uerc uuldurfadur,
	    sue he uundra gihuaes,
		work-of glory-father,
		    as he wonder each,
			the work of the glorious father,
			    as he of each wonder

4	eci dryctin,
	    or astelidæ.
		eternal lord,
		    origin established.
			eternal lord,
			    the origin established.

5	He aerist scop
	    aelda barnum
		He first created
		    elders' children
			He first created
			    for the children of elders

6	heben til hrofe,
	    haleg scepen;
		heaven for a-roof,
		    holy shaper;
			heaven for a roof,
			    holy shaper;

7	tha middungeard
	    moncynnæs uard,
		then middle-earth
		    mankind's ward,
			then middle-earth
			    mandkind's guardian

8	eci dryctin,
	    æfter tiadæ
		eternal lord,
		    after titled
			eternal lord,
			    after titled

9	firum foldu,
	    frea allmectig.
		for-men lands,
		    lord almighty.
			the lands for men,
			    lord almighty.

Word List

Ænglisc	English	*Ænglisc*	English
æfter	after	maecti	might
aelda	elders'	metudæs	the-measurer's
aerist	first	middungeard	middle-earth
allmectig	almighty	modgidanc	mind-plans
astelidæ	established	moncynnæs	mankind's
barnum	children	Nu	now
dryctin	lord	or	origin
eci	eternal	scepen	shaper
end	and	scop	created
firum	for-men	scylun	shall-we
foldu	lands	sue	as
frea	lord	tha	then
gihuaes	each	tiadæ	titled
haleg	holy	til	for
he	he	uard	ward
heben	heaven	uerc	work-of
hefaenricaes	heaven-kingdom's	uuldurfadur	glory-father
hergan	honour	uundra	wonder
his	his		
hrofe	a-roof		

3.9 Caedmon's Hymn (West Saxon Version)

Text

	Ænglisc	Literal	English
1	*Nu sculon herigean*	Now shall-we honour	Now shall we honour
	heofonrices weard,	heaven-kingdom's ward,	the guardian of heaven,
2	*meotodes meahte*	the-measurer's might	the meaurer's might
	and his modgeþanc,	and his mind-plans,	and his mind's design,
3	*weorc wuldorfæder,*	work-of glory-father,	the work of the glorious father,
	swa he wundra gehwæs,	as he wonder each,	as he of each wonder
4	*ece drihten,*	eternal lord,	eternal lord,
	or onstealde.	origin established.	the origin established.
5	*He ærest sceop*	He first created	He first created
	eorðan bearnum	elders' children	for the children of elders
6	*heofon to hrofe,*	heaven for a-roof,	heaven for a roof,
	halig scyppend;	holy shaper;	holy shaper;
7	*þa middangeard*	then middle-earth	then middle-earth
	moncynnes weard,	mankind's ward,	mandkind's guardian
8	*ece drihten,*	eternal lord,	eternal lord,
	æfter teode	after titled	after titled
9	*firum foldan,*	for-men lands,	the lands for men,
	frea ælmihtig.	lord almighty.	lord almighty.

Word List

Ænglisc	English	*Ænglisc*	English
æfter	after	*meotodes*	the-measurer's
ælmihtig	almighty	*middangeard*	middle-earth
ærest	first	*modgeþanc*	mind-plans
and	and	*moncynnes*	mankind's
bearnum	children	*Nu*	now
drihten	lord	*onstealde*	established
ece	eternal	*or*	origin
eorðan	elders'	*sceop*	created
firum	for-men	*sculon*	shall-we
foldan	lands	*scyppend*	shaper
frea	lord	*swa*	as
gehwæs	each	*teode*	titled
halig	holy	*þa*	then
he	he	*to*	for
heofon	heaven	*weard*	ward
heofonrices	heaven-kingdom's	*weorc*	work-of
herigean	honour	*wuldorfæder*	glory-father
his	his	*wundra*	wonder
hrofe	a-roof		
meahte	might		

3.10 Thureth

Text

	Ænglisc	Literal	English

1	*Ic eom halgungboc;*
	    healde hine dryhten
		I am holy-book;
		    hold he the-lord
			I am of the holy book;
			    may the lord keep him

2	*þe me fægere þus*
	    frætewum belegde.
		that me beautifully thus
		    ornaments covered.
			that has beautifully
			    covered me in ornaments.

3	*þureð to þance*
	    þus het me wyrcean,
		Thureth to thank
		    thus ordered me created,
			Thureth thankfully
			    thus ordered me to be created,

4	*to loue and to wurðe,*
	    þam þe leoht gesceop.
		to love and to worth,
		    them that light created.
			to love and honour,
			    he who created the light.

5	*Gemyndi is he*
	    mihta gehwylcre
		Mindful is he
		    mighty works
			He is minfdul
			    of all the mighty works

6	*þæs þe he on foldan*
	    gefremian mæg,
		so that he on earth
		    accomplish may,
			which he on earth
			    is able to accomplish,

7	*and him geþancie*
	    þeoda waldend
		and him thank
		    nations ruler
			and he shall be thanked
			    by the ruler of nations

8	*þæs þe he on gemynde*
	    madma manega
		so that he in mindful
		    treasures many
			because he, mindful
			    of many treasures

9	*wyle gemearcian*
	    metode to lace;
		wishes to-mark
		    the-Creator to offer;
			wishes to mark me
			    as an offering to the creator;

10	*and he sceal æce lean*
	    ealle findan
		and he shall eternal reward
		    all find
			and he shall eternal reward
			    fully obtain,

11	*þæs þe he on foldan*
	    fremaþ to ryhte.
		so that he on earth
		    acts forth properly.
			because he on earth
			    acts here properly.

Word List

Ænglisc	English	*Ænglisc*	English
æce	eternal	*gemynde*	mindful
and	and	*gemyndi*	mindful
belegde	covered	*gesceop*	created
dryhten	the-lord	*geþancie*	thank
ealle	all	*halgungboc*	holy-book
eom	am	*he*	he
fægere	beautifully	*healde*	hold
findan	find	*het*	ordered
foldan	earth	*him*	him
frætewum	ornaments	*hine*	he
fremaþ	acts	*ic*	I
gefremian	accomplish	*is*	is
gehwylcre	works	*lace*	offer
gemearcian	to-mark	*lean*	reward

Ænglisc	English
leoht	light
loue	love
madma	treasures
mæg	may
manega	many
me	me
metode	the-Creator, the-Creator
mihta	mighty
on	in
on	on
ryhte	properly
sceal	shall
þæs	so
þam	them
þance	thank
þe	that
þeoda	nations
þureð	Thureth
þus	thus
to	to
waldend	ruler
wurðe	worth
wyle	wishes
wyrcean	created

3.11 Aldhelm

Text

Ænglisc	Literal	English
1 *þus me gesette*	thus me composed	Thus he composed me
sanctus et iustus	saintly and just	the saintly and just
2 *beorn boca gleaw,*	nobleman of books learned,	nobleman learned of books,
bonus auctor,	a good author,	a good author,
3 *Ealdelm, æþele sceop,*	Aldhelm, a noble poet,	Aldhelm, a noble poet,
etiam fuit	also he was	also he was
4 *ipselos on æðele*	high in nobility	high in nobility
Angolsexna,	of the Anglo-Saxons,	of the Anglo-Saxons,
5 *byscop on Bretene.*	a bishop in Britain.	a bishop in Britain.
Biblos ic nu sceal,	The book I now shall,	The book I shall now,
6 *ponus et pondus*	work and weight	a work of weight
pleno cum sensu,	full with sense,	with full sense,
7 *geonges geanoðe*	youth's meeting	with youth meeting
geomres iamiamque,	mournful right now,	mournfully right now,
8 *secgan soð, nalles leas,*	tell truly, not at all false,	tell all truly, and not at all falsely,
þæt him symle wæs	that he always to be	that he always had
9 *euthenia*	prosperity	prosperity
oftor on fylste,	often in support,	often supported
10 *æne on eðle*	at once in homeland	at once in his himeland
ec ðon ðe se is	though than that he is	even though he is
11 *yfel on gesæd.*	badly of spoken.	badly spoken of.
Etiam nusquam	Also never	Also never
12 *ne sceal ladigan*	nor should excuse	nor should excuse
labor quem tenet	work who holds	work who holds
13 *encratea,*	power-inside,	mastery,
ac he ealneg sceal	but he always shall	but he shall always
14 *boethia*	Boethius	Boethius
biddan georne	ask eagerly	ask eagerly
15 *þurh his modes gemind*	for the sake of his mind's thoughts	for the sake of his mind's thoughts
micro in cosmo,	little in the world,	little in the world,
16 *þæt him drihten gyfe*	that he the Lord gave	that he the Lord gave
dinamis on eorðan,	power on earth,	power on earth
17 *fortis factor,*	strength maker,	strength maker,
þæt he forð simle	that he forth ever	that he forth forever.

Word List

Ænglisc	English	Ænglisc	English
ac	but	him	he
æðele	nobility	his	his
æne	at once	iamiamque	right now (Latin)
æþele	a noble	ic	I
angolsexna	of the Anglo-Saxons	in	in
auctor	author (Latin)	ipselos	high (Latin)
beorn	nobleman	is	is
biblos	the book (Latin)	iustus	just (Latin)
biddan	ask	labor	work
boca	of books	ladigan	excuse
boethia	Boethius	leas	false
bonus	a good	me	me
bretene	Britain	micro	little (Latin)
byscop	a bishop	modes	mind's
cosmo	the world	nalles	not at all
cum	with (Latin)	ne	nor
ðe	that	nu	now
dinamis	powerful (Latin)	nusquam	never (Latin)
ðon	than	oftor	often
drihten	the Lord	on	in
ealdelm	Aldhelm	on	of
ealneg	always	on	on
ec	other	pleno	full (Latin)
eðle	homeland	pondus	weight (Latin)
encratea	power-inside	ponus	work (Latin)
eorðan	earth	quem	who (Latin)
et	and	sanctus	saintly
etiam	also (Latin)	sceal	shall
euthenia	prosperity	sceal	should
factor	maker (Latin)	sceop	poet
forð	forth	se	he
fortis	strength (Latin)	secgan	tell
fuit	he was (Latin)	sensu	sense (Latin)
fylste	support	simle	ever
geanoðe	meeting	soð	truly
gemind	thoughts	symle	always
geomres	mournful	tenet	holds (Latin)
geonges	youth's	þæt	that
georne	eagerly	þurh	for the sake of
gesæd	spoken	þus	thus
gesette	composed	wæs	to be
gleaw	learned	yfel	badly
gyfe	gave		
he	he		

3.12 Durham

Text

Ænglisc	Literal	English
1	*Is ðeos burch breome geond Breotenrice,*	Is this city famous over Britain-kingdom,	This city is famous over the Kingdom of Britain,
2	*steppa gestaðolad, stanas ymbutan*	steps founded, stones about	with steps founded with stones about
3	*wundrum gewæxen. Weor ymbeornad,*	wondrously grown. The Wear beholds,	wondrously grown. The Wear beholds,
4	*ea yðum stronge, and ðer inne wunað*	river waves strong, and there in dwell	a river of strong waves, and therein dwell
5	*feola fisca kyn on floda gemonge.*	many fish kinds in flood together.	many kinds of fish in the floods together.
6	*And ðær gewexen is wudafæstern micel;*	And there grown is wood-fastened great;	And there is grown great forests;
7	*wuniad in ðem wycum wilda deor monige,*	live in they dwellings wild beasts many,	There living in the dwellings many wild beasts,
8	*in deope dalum deora ungerim.*	in deep dales deer innumerable.	in deep dales inumerable deer.
9	*Is in ðere byri eac bearnum gecyðed*	Is in this city also children well-known	Also in this city well known to children of men
10	*ðe arfesta eadig Cudberch*	the merciful blessed Cuthbert	the merciful blessed Cuthbert
11	*and ðes clene cyninges heafud,*	and this clean king's head,	and this chaste king's head,
12	*Osuualdes, Engle leo, and Aidan biscop,*	Oswald's, Angli lion, and Aidan bishop,	Oswald, the lion of the Angli, and Biship Aidan,
13	*Eadberch and Eadfrið, æðele geferes.*	Eadbert and Eadfrid, noble associates.	Eadbert and Eadfrid, the noble associates.
14	*Is ðer inne midd heom*	Is there in the middle with them	There in among them
	æðelwold biscop	Aethelwold bishop	Bishop Aethelwold
15	*and breoma bocera Beda,*	and celebrated writer of books Bede,	and celebrated writer of books Bede,
	and Boisil abbot,	and Boisil abbot,	and Abbot Boisil,
16	*ðe clene Cudberte on gecheðe*	as clean Cuthbert in youth	as chaste Cuthbert in youth
17	*lerde lustum, and he his lara wel genom.*	learned joyfully, and he his learning well took.	learned joyfully, and he took his learning well.
18	*Eardiæð æt ðem eadige in in ðem minstre*	Inhabited at these blessed in the-chamber these ministers	Inhabited these blessed chamber these ministers
19	*unarimeda*	unnumbered	unnumbered

Ænglisc	Literal	English
reliquia,	relics,	relics,
20 *ðær monia wundrum gewurðað,*	that many wondrous being,	that many being wondrous,
ðes ðe writ seggeð,	these that writings say,	so the writings say,
21 *midd ðene drihnes wer domes bideð.*	with the Lord's man judgement awaits.	with the Lord's people judgement awaits.

Word List

Ænglisc	English	Ænglisc	English
abbot	abbot	*ðere*	this
æðele	noble	*ðes*	these
æðelwold	Aethelwold	*ðes*	this
æt	at	*domes*	judgement
aidan	Aidan	*drihnes*	Lord's
and	and	*ea*	river
arfesta	merciful	*eac*	also
bearnum	children	*eadberch*	Eadbert
beda	Bede	*eadfrið*	Eadfrid
bideð	awaits	*eadig*	blessed
biscop	bishop	*eadige*	blessed
bocera	writer of books	*eardiæð*	inhabited
boisil	Boisil	*engle*	Angli
breoma	celebrated	*feola*	many
breome	famous	*fisca*	fish
breotenrice	Britain-kingdom	*floda*	flood
burch	city	*gecheðe*	youth
byri	city	*gecyðed*	well-known
clene	clean	*geferes*	associates
cudberch	Cuthbert	*gemonge*	together
cudberte	Cuthbert	*genom*	took
cyninges	king's	*geond*	over
ðær	that	*gestaðolad*	founded
ðær	there	*gewæxen*	grown
dalum	dales	*gewexen*	grown
ðe	as	*gewurðað*	being
ðe	that	*he*	he
ðe	the	*heafud*	head
ðem	these	*heom*	with them
ðem	they	*his*	his
ðene	the	*in*	in
deope	deep	*in*	the-chamber
deor	beasts	*inne*	in
deora	deer	*is*	is
ðeos	this	*kyn*	kinds
ðer	there	*lara*	learning

Ænglisc	English
leo	lion
lerde	learned
lustum	joyfully
micel	great
midd	the middle
midd	with
minstre	ministers
monia	many
monige	many
on	in
osuualdes	Oswald's
reliquia	relics
seggeð	say
stanas	stones
steppa	steps
stronge	strong
unarimeda	unnumbered
ungerim	innumerable
wel	well
weor	the Wear
wer	man
wilda	wild
writ	writings
wudafæstern	wood-fastened
wunað	dwell
wundrum	wondrous
wundrum	wondrously
wuniad	live
wycum	dwellings
yðum	waves
ymbeornad	beholds
ymbutan	about

3.13 A Summons to Prayer

Text

	Ænglisc	Literal	English
1	*þænne gemiltsað þe, N.,*	then have mercy you, (name),	Then he will have mercy upon you, (name),
	mundum qui regit,	the world who rules,	who rules the world,
2	*ðeoda þrymcyningc*	nations the ruling king	the ruling king of nations
	thronum sedentem	the throne sitting on	sitting on the throne
3	*a butan ende*	a without end	without end
4	*saule þinre*	soul yours	your soul
5	*Geunne þe on life*	Grant you in life	May he grant you in life
	auctor pacis	author of peace	the author of peace
6	*sibbe gesælða,*	joys of peace,	the joys of peace,
	salus mundi,	salvation of the world,	the salvation of the world,
7	*metod se mæra*	creator the famous	the famous creator
	magna uirtute,	great virtue,	of great virtue,
8	*and se soðfæsta*	and the truth-fastened	and righteous
	summi filius	highest son	the highest son
9	*fo on fultum,*	receive in comfort,	receive (you) in comfort,
	factor cosmi,	maker of the world,	the maker of the world,
10	*se of æþelre wæs*	who of noble was	who was of noble
	uirginis partu	maiden birth	maiden birth
11	*clæne acenned*	clean born	born chaste
	Christus in orbem,	Christ into the world,	Christ to the world,
12	*metod þurh Marian,*	creator through Mary,	the creator through Mary,
	mundi redemptor,	the world's redeemer,	the world's redeemer,
13	*and þurh þæne halgan gast.*	and through the holy spirit.	and through the holy spirit.
	Uoca frequenter	Call frequently	Call frequently
14	*bide helpes hine,*	pray for help him,	pray to him for help,
	clemens deus,	clement God,	clement God,
15	*se onsended wæs*	who sent was	who was sent
	summo de throno	highest of thrones	from the highest of thrones
16	*and þære clænan*	and to the clean	and to the chaste
	clara uoce	clear voice	clear voice
17	*þa gebyrd bodade*	the birth heralded	the birth heralded
	bona uoluntate	good will	of good will
18	*þæt heo scolde cennan*	that she should bear	that she should bear
	Christum regem,	Christ the king,	Christ the king,
19	*ealra cyninga cyningc,*	all kings king of,	the king of all kings,
	casta uiuendo.	chaste living.	of chaste living.
20	*and þu þa soðfæstan*	And you as truth-fastened	And you as righteous
	supplex rogo,	supplicant pray,	supplicant pray,
21	*fultumes bidde friclo*	eagerly ask aid	ask eagerly for aid
	uirginem almum,	the virgin nurturing,	from the nurturing virgin,
22	*and þær æfter to*	and there after to	and there after to

	Ænglisc / Latin	English	English
	omnes sancti	all the saints	all the saints
23	*bliðmod bidde,*	blithe-minded pray,	gentle-minded pray,
	beatus et iustus,	blessed and just,	blessed and just,
24	*þæt hi ealle þe*	that they all for you	that they all for you
	unica uoce	one voice	with one voice
25	*þingian to þeodne*	intercede to the prince	intercede to the prince
	thronum regentem,	the throne ruling,	ruling the throne,
26	*æcum drihtne,*	eternal lord,	eternal lord,
	alta polorum,	heights of the poles,	the heights of the heavens,
27	*þæt he þine saule,*	that he your soul,	that he your soul,
	summus iudex,	highest judge,	the highest judge,
28	*onfo freolice,*	receive freely,	receive freely,
	factor aeternus,	maker eternal,	the eternal creator,
29	*and he gelæde*	and he leads	and he leads
	luce perhennem,	light perpetual,	into eternal light,
30	*þær eadige*	there blessed	there where blessed
	animæ sanctæ	souls holy	holy souls
31	*rice restað*	kingdom rest	rest in the kingdom,
	regna caelorum.	kingdom of heaven.	the kingdom of heaven.

Word List

Ænglisc	English	Ænglisc	English
a	a	*clæne*	clean
acenned	born	*clara*	clear (Latin)
æcum	eternal	*clemens*	clement (Latin)
æfter	after	*cosmi*	of the world (Latin)
aeternus	eternal (Latin)	*cyninga*	kings
æþelre	noble	*cyningc*	king of
almum	nurturing (Latin)	*de*	of (Latin)
alta	heights	*ðeoda*	nations
and	and	*deus*	god (Latin)
animæ	souls (Latin)	*drihtne*	lord
auctor	author (Latin)	*eadige*	blessed
beatus	blessed (Latin)	*ealle*	all
bidde	ask	*ealra*	all
bidde	pray	*ende*	end
bide	pray	*et*	and (Latin)
bliðmod	blithe-minded	*factor*	maker (Latin)
bodade	heralded	*filius*	son (Latin)
bona	good (Latin)	*fo*	receive
butan	without	*freolice*	freely
caelorum	of heaven (Latin)	*frequenter*	frequently (Latin)
casta	chaste	*friclo*	aid
cennan	bear	*fultum*	comfort
christum	Christ (Latin)	*fultumes*	eagerly
christus	Christ (Latin)	*gast*	spirit
clænan	clean	*gebyrd*	birth

Ænglisc	English	*Ænglisc*	English
gelæde	leads	*scolde*	should
gemiltsað	have mercy	*se*	the
gesælða	of peace	*se*	who
geunne	grant	*sedentem*	sitting on (Latin)
halgan	holy	*sibbe*	joys
he	he	*soðfæsta*	truth-fastened
helpes	for help	*soðfæstan*	truth-fastened
heo	she	*summi*	highest (Latin)
hi	they	*summo*	highest (Latin)
hine	him	*summus*	highest (Latin)
in	into	*supplex*	supplicant (Latin)
iudex	judge (Latin)	*þa*	as
iustus	just (Latin)	*þa*	the
life	life	*þæne*	the
luce	light (Latin)	*þænne*	then
mæra	famous	*þær*	there
magna	great (Latin)	*þære*	to the
marian	Mary	*þæt*	that
metod	creator	*þe*	for you
mundi	of the world (Latin)	*þe*	you
mundi	the world's (Latin)	*þeodne*	the prince
mundum	the world (Latin)	*þine*	your
n	(name)	*þingian*	intercede
of	of	*þinre*	yours
omnes	all (Latin)	*throno*	thrones
on	in	*thronum*	the throne
onfo	receive	*thronum*	the throne
onsended	sent	*þrymcyningc*	the ruling king
orbem	the world (Latin)	*þu*	you
pacis	of peace (Latin)	*þurh*	through
partu	birth	*to*	to
perhennem	perpetual	*uirginem*	the virgin (Latin)
polorum	of the poles (Latin)	*uirginis*	maiden (Latin)
qui	who (Latin)	*uirtute*	virtue (Latin)
redemptor	redeemer (Latin)	*uiuendo*	living (Latin)
regem	the king (Latin)	*unica*	one (Latin)
regentem	ruling (Latin)	*uoca*	call (Latin)
regit	rules (Latin)	*uoce*	voice (Latin)
regna	kingdom (Latin)	*uoluntate*	will (Latin)
restað	rest	*wæs*	was
rice	kingdom		
rogo	pray (Latin)		
salus	salvation (Latin)		
sanctæ	holy (Latin)		
sancti	the saints (Latin)		
saule	soul		

3.14 Waldere B

Text

	Ænglisc	Literal	English
1	"mece bæteran	"Sword better	"a better sword
2	buton ðam anum	except the one	except the one
	ðe ic eac hafa	which I also have	which I also have
3	on stanfate	in jewelled-sheath	in a jewelled sheath
	stille gehided.	quietly hidden.	quietly hidden.
4	Ic wat þæt hit ðohte	I know that of it thought	I know that of it thought
	ðeodric Widian	Theodric to Widia	Theodric to Widia
5	selfum onsendon,	himself to send,	himself to send,
	and eac sinc micel	and also riches many	and also many riches
6	maðma mid ði mece,	treasure with the sword,	treasure with the sword,
	monig oðres mid him	many other with it	many others with it
7	golde gegirwan	gold adorned	gold adorned
	(iulean genam),	(reward taken),	(the reward was taken),
8	þæs ðe hine of nearwum	because of him from captivity	because of him from captivity
	Niðhades mæg,	Nithad's kinsman,	Nithhad's kinsman,
9	Welandes bearn,	Weland's son,	Weland's son,
	Widia ut forlet;	Widia out released;	Widia released (him);
10	ðurh fifela geweald	through a monster's domain	through the domain of a monster
	forð onette".	forth hasten".	hasten forth".
11	Waldere maðelode,	Waldere spoke,	Waldere spoke,
	wiga ellenrof,	warrior courageous,	the courageous warrior,
12	hæfde him on handa	had he in hands	he had in his hands
	hildefrofre,	weapon,	the battle-comfort (weapon),
13	guðbilla gripe,	battle-bill gripped,	battle-bill (blade) in his grip,
	gyddode wordum:	spoke words:	he spoke the words:
14	Hwæt! ðu huru wendest,	"Indeed! you surely expected,	"Indeed! you surely expected,
	wine Burgenda,	friend Of the Burgundians,	friend of the Burgundians,
15	þæt me Hagenan hand	that me Hagen's hand	that against me Hagen's hand
	hilde gefremede	battle prevail	would prevail in battle
16	and getwæmde feðewigges.	and separate foot-battle.	and separate me from the fray.
	Feta, gyf ðu dyrre,	Take, if you dare,	Take, if you dare,
17	æt ðus heaðuwerigan	from me thus battle-weary	from me thus battle-weary
	hare byrnan.	grey armour.	the grey armour.
18	Standeð me her on eaxelum	Stands on me here about shoulders	It stands here on my shoulders
	ælfheres laf,	Ælfhere's legacy,	Ælfhere's legacy,
19	god and geapneb,	good and cleverly-woven,	good and cleverly woven,
	golde geweorðod,	gold adorned,	adorned with gold
20	ealles unscende	all blameless	a wholly blameless
	æðelinges reaf	noble's vestment	prince's vestment

	Ænglisc	Literal	English

21	to habbanne,
	    þonne hand wereð
		to have,
		    when hand protects
			to have,
			    when his hand protects

22	feorhhord feondum.	his soul-hoard his enemies.	his soul-hoard from his enemies.
	Ne bið fah wið me,	Not be hostile against me,	It will not be hostile to me,

23	þonne me unmægas
	    eft ongynnað,
		when to me unrelated
		    again assail,
			when men unrelated
			    again assail,

24	mecum gemetað,
	    swa ge me dydon.
		sword meet with,
		    as you me did.
			meet me with swords,
			    as you did to me.

25	ðeah mæg sige syllan
	    se ðe symle byð
		yet may victory give
		    he who always be
			Yet he may give victory,
			    he who is ever

26	recon and rædfest
	    ryhta gehwilces.
		ready and sound
		    rights matters
			ready and sound in council
			    in every matter of right

27	Se ðe him to ðam halgan
	    helpe gelifeð,
		He that the to the holy one
		    help trusts,
			He who to that holy one
			    trusts for help,

28	to gode gioce,
	    he þær gearo findeð
		to God's support,
		    he there ready finds
			to God for support,
			    he finds it ready there

29	gif ða earnunga
	    ær geðenceð.
		if that earning
		    first considers.
			if he has earnt it
			    first he considers.

30	þonne moten wlance
	    welan britnian,
		then may the proud
		    wealth dispense,
			They may the proud
			    dispense wealth,

31	æhtum wealdan,
	    þæt is..."
		possessions rule over,
		    that is..."
			rule over possessions,
			    that is..."

Word List

Ænglisc	English	Ænglisc	English
æðelinges	noble's	ðe	which
æhtum	possessions	ðe	who
ælfheres	Ælfhere's	ðeah	yet
ær	first	ðeodric	Theodric
æt	from me	ði	the
and	and	ðohte	thought
anum	one	ðu	you
bæteran	better	ðurh	through
bearn	son	ðus	thus
bið	be	dydon.	did
britnian	dispense	dyrre	dare
burgenda	of the Burgundians	eac	also
buton	except	ealles	all
byð	be	earnunga	earning
byrnan.	armour	eaxelum	shoulders
ða	that	eft	again
ðam	the	ellenrof	courageous
ðe	of	fah	hostile
ðe	that	feðewigges	foot-battle

Ænglisc	English	Ænglisc	English
feondum.	his enemies	him	he
feorhhord	soul-hoard	him	it
feta	take	him	the
fifela	a monster's	hine	him
findeð	finds	hit	of it
forð	forth	huru	surely
forlet;	released	hwæt	indeed
ge	you	ic	I
geapneb	cleverly-woven	is	is
gearo	ready	iulean	reward
geðenceð.	considers	laf	legacy
gefremede	prevail	maðelode	spoke
gegirwan	adorned	maðma	treasure
gehided.	hidden	mæg	kinsman
gehwilces	matters	mæg	may
gelifeð	trusts	me	me
gemetað	meet with	me	on me
genam	taken	me	to me
getwæmde	separate	mece	Sword
geweald	domain	mecum	sword
geweorðod	adorned	micel	many
gif	if	mid	with
gioce	support	monig	many
god	good	moten	may
God's	God's	ne	not
golde	gold	nearwum	captivity
gripe	gripped	niðhades	Nithad's
guðbilla	battle-bill	oðres	other
gyddode	spoke	of	from
gyf	if	on	about
habbanne	have	on	in
hæfde	had	onette	hasten
hafa	have	ongynnað	assail
hagenan	Hagen's	onsendon	to send
halgan	holy one	rædfest	sound
hand	hand	reaf	vestment
handa	hands	recon	ready
hare	grey	rhyta	rights
he	he	se	he
heaðuwerigan	battle-weary	selfum	himself
helpe	help	sige	victory
her	here	sinc	riches
hilde	battle	standeð	stands
hildefrofre	weapon	stanfate	jewelled-sheath

Ænglisc	English
stille	quietly
swa	as
syllan	give
symle	always
þær	there
þæs	because
þæt	that
þonne	then
þonne	when
to	to
unmægas	unrelated
unscende	blameless
ut	out
waldere	Waldere
wat	know
wealdan	rule over
welan	wealth
welandes	Weland's
wendest	expected
wereð	protects
wið	against
widia	Widia
widian	to Widia
wiga	warrior
wine	friend
wlance	the proud
wordum	words

4 The Exeter Book

4.1 Pharaoh

Text

	Ænglisc	Literal	English
1	*"Saga me hwæt þær weorudes*	"Tell me what there troops	"Tell me what troops there were
	wære ealles	were all	which were all
2	*on Farones fyrde,*	in Pharoah's army,	in the Pharoah's army,
	þa hy folc godes	when they folk heathen-god's	when they the heathen-god's folk
3	*þurh feondscipe*	sake-of enmity	for the sake of enmity
	fylgan ongunn...."	pursued undertake...."	undertook to pursue…"
4	*"Nat ic hit be wihte,*	"Not I it about anything,	"I do not know anythng about it,
	butan ic wene þus,	except I think thus,	except that I think,
5	*þæt þær screoda wære*	that there numbered were	that there were numbered,
	gescyred rime	alloted counted	alloted and counted
6	*siex hun... ...a*	six hundred… …all	six hundred… …all
	searohæbbendra;	armoured;	armoured;
7	*þæt eal fornam*	that all swept-away	that were swept away
	yþ...	wave…	by a wave…
8	*wraþe wyrde*	wrathfully destroyed	wrathfully destroyed
	in woruldrice".	in world-kingdom".	in the kingdom of the world".

Word List

Ænglisc	English	*Ænglisc*	English
a	all	*hy*	they
be	about	*ic*	I
butan	except	*in*	in
eal	all	*me*	me
ealles	all	*nat*	not
Farones	Pharoah's	*on*	in
feondscipe	enmity	*ongunn*	undertake
folc	folk	*rime*	counted
fornam	swept-away	*saga*	tell
fylgan	pursued	*screoda*	numbered
fyrde	army	*searohæbbendra*	armoured
gescyred	alloted	*siex*	six
godes	God-heathen's	*þa*	when
hit	it	*þær*	there
hun	hundred	*þæt*	that
hwæt	what	*þurh*	sake-of

Ænglisc	English
þus	thus
wære	were
wene	think
weorudes	troops
wihte	anything
woruldrice	world-kingdom
wraþe	wrathfully
wyrde	destroyed
yþ	wave

4.2 Alms-Giving

Text

Ænglisc	Literal	English
1　*Wel bið þam eorle*	Well being that earl	Well will it be for the earl
þe him on innan hafað,	that he in within has,	that he has within him,
2　*reþehygdig wer,*	right-thinking man,	a right-thinking man,
rume heortan;	roomy heart;	a roomy heart;
3　*þæt him biþ for worulde*	that he be for the-world	that will be for him in the world
weorðmynda mæst,	worth-minded most,	the most worthy,
4　*ond for ussum dryhtne*	and for us the-lord	and before us the lord
doma selast.	deeming excellence.	of excellent judgements.
5　*Efne swa he mid wætre*	Even as he with water	Even as he with water
þone weallendan	then welling	then welling
6　*leg adwæsce,*	lays quenched,	lays quenched,
þæt he leng ne mæg	that it longer not may	that it no longer may
7　*blac byrnende*	bright burning	brightly burning
burgum sceððan,	cities harm,	harming cities,
8　*swa he mid ælmessan*	so he with alms	so he with alms
ealle toscufeð	all do-away	will do away with all
9　*synna wunde,*	sin wounds,	wounds of sin,
sawla lacnað.	souls healed.	and heal souls.

Word List

Ænglisc	English	*Ænglisc*	English
adwæsce	quenched	leg	lays
ælmessan	alms	leng	longer
bið	being	mæg	may
biþ	be	mæst	most
blac	bright	mid	with
burgum	cities	ne	not
byrnende	burning	on	in
doma	deeming	ond	and
dryhtne	the-lord	reþehygdig	right-thinking
ealle	all	rume	roomy
efne	even	sawla	souls
eorle	earl	sceððan	harm
for	for	selast	excellence
hafað	has	swa	as
he	he	swa	so
he	it	synna	sin
heortan	heart	þæt	that
him	he	þam	that
innan	within	þe	that
lacnað	healed	þone	then

Ænglisc	English
toscufeð	do-away
ussum	us
wætre	water
weallendan	welling
wel	well
weorðmynda	worth-minded
wer	man
worulde	the-world
wunde	wounds

4.3   The Lord's Prayer I

Text

Ænglisc	Literal	English
1 ...g fæder,	...g father,	...g father,
þu þe on heofonum eardast,	you that in heaven dwell,	you that dwell in heaven,
2 geweorðad wuldres dreame.	make worthy wondrous rejoicing.	make worthy wondrous rejoicing.
Sy þinum weorcum halgad	Be your work hallowed	Be your deeds hallowed
3 noma niþþa bearnum;	the name men son;	in the name of men your son;
þu eart nergend wera.	you are saviour of man.	you who are the saviour of man.
4 Cyme þin rice wide,	Come your kingdom wide,	May your wide kingdom come,
ond þin rædfæst willa	and your righteous will	and your righteous will
5 aræred under rodores hrofe,	raise under the heavens a roof,	raise a roof under the heavens,
eac þon on rumre foldan.	also then in wide earth.	beside the wide earth.
6 Syle us to dæge	Give us to day	Give us today
domfæstne blæd,	judgement-firm glory	the glory of your true judgement
7 hlaf userne,	bread ours,	our bread,
helpend wera,	help man,	help men,
8 þone singalan,	those continuously,	those continuously,
soðfæst meotod.	truth-firm creator.	true creator.
9 Ne læt usic costunga	Do not allow us temptation	Do not let us into temptation
cnyssan to swiðe,	drive forth exceedingly,	drive forth exceedingly,
10 ac þu us freodom gief,	nevertheless you us freedom give,	though you give us freedom,
folca waldend,	folk ruler,	ruler of the people,
11 from yfla gehwam,	away evil every,	away from all evil,
a to widan feore.	eternity to from life.	from life to eternity.

Word List

Ænglisc	English	*Ænglisc*	English
a	always	eac	also
ac	nevertheless	eardast	dwell
aræred	raise	eart	be
bearnum	son	fæder	father
blæd	glory	feore	life
cnyssan	drive	folca	folk
costunga	temptation	foldan	earth
cyme	come	freodom	freedom
dæge	day	from	away
domfæstne	judgement-firm	gehwam	every
dreame	rejoicing	geweorðad	give worthiness to

Ænglisc	English
gief	give
halgad	hallowed
helpend	help
heofonum	heaven
hlaf	bread
hrofe	a roof
læt	allow
meotod	creator
ne	do not
nergend	saviour
niþþa	men
noma	the name
on	in
ond	and
rædfæst	righteous
rice	kingdom
rodores	the heavens
rumre	wide
singalan	continuously
soðfæst	truth-firm
swiðe	exceedingly
sy	be
syle	give
þe	that
þin	your
þinum	your
þon	then
þone	those
þu	you
to	to
to	forth
under	under
us	us
userne	ours
usic	us
waldend	ruler
weorcum	work
wera	of man
wera	man
widan	wide
wide	wide
willa	will
wuldres	wondrous
yfla	evil

4.4   The Partridge

Text

Ænglisc	Literal	English
1 *Hyrde ic secgan gen*	Heard I told yet	I have yet heard told
bi sumum fugle	about a-certain bird	about a certain bird
2 *wundorlicne*	wondrous	wondrous
3 *fæger,*	fair,	fair,
4 *þæt word þe gecwæð*	that word that said	is the word that was said
wuldres ealdor:	glory lord:	by the Lord of Glory:
5 *In swa hwylce tiid*	"In so such time	"In such time
swa ge mid treowe to me	as you with faith to me	as you have faith with me
6 *on hyge hweorfað,*	in soul turn,	and turn with your soul,
ond ge hellfirena	and you hell-fire-like	and you hell-fire
7 *sweartra geswicað,*	darkness abandon,	and darkness abandon,
swa ic symle to eow	so I forever to you	so I forever to you
8 *mid siblufan*	with love	with love
sona gecyrre	at once turn	at once will turn
9 *þurh milde mod.*	by merciful heart.	by merciful heart.
Ge beoð me siþþan	You shall be to me thenceforth	You shall be to be then
10 *torhte tireadge*	bright glorious	bright glorious
talade ond rimde,	numbered and the host,	numbered with the heavenly host,
11 *beorhte gebroþor*	bright brethren	bright brethren
on bearna stæl.	in children's place of".	instead of children".
12 *Uton we þy geornor*	Let us we by this gladly	Let us by this gladly
gode oliccan,	god praise,	praise god,
13 *firene feogan,*	sin hating,	hating sin,
friþes earnian,	peace earning,	earning peace,
14 *duguðe to dryhtne,*	virtue to the Lord,	virtue to the Lord,
þenden us dæg scine,	so long as upon us the day shines,	so long as they day shines upon us,
15 *þæt swa æþelne*	that as nobler	that nobler
eardwica cyst	dwelling place choice	dwelling place we choose
16 *in wuldres wlite*	in wondrous beauty	in wondrous beauty
wunian motan.	dwelling be allowed to.	to be allowed to dwell.
17 *Finit.*	The end.	The end.

Word List

Ænglisc	English	*Ænglisc*	English
æþelne	nobler	*cyst*	choice
bearna	children's	*dæg*	the day
beoð	shall be	*dryhtne*	the Lord
beorhte	bright	*duguðe*	virtue
bi	about	*ealdor*	lord

Ænglisc	English	Ænglisc	English
eardwica	dwelling place	þæt	that
earnian	earning	þe	that
eow	you	þenden	so long as
fæger	fair	þurh	by
feogan	hating	þy	by this
finit	the end	tiid	time
firene	sin	tireadge	glorious
friþes	peace	to	to
fugle	bird	torhte	bright
ge	you	treowe	faith
gebroþor	brethren	us	upon us
gecwæð	said	uton	let us
gecyrre	turn	we	we
gen	yet	wlite	beauty
geornor	gladly	word	word
geswicað	abandon	wuldres	glory
gode	god	wuldres	wondrous
hellfirena	hell-fire-like	wundorlicne	wondrous
hweorfað	turn	wunian	dwelling
hwylce	such		
hyge	soul		
hyrde	heard		
ic	I		
in	in		
me	me		
me	to me		
mid	with		
milde	merciful		
mod	heart		
motan	be allowed to		
oliccan	praise		
on	in		
ond	and		
rimde	the host		
scine	shines		
secgan	told		
siblufan	love		
siþþan	thenceforth		
sona	at once		
stæl	place of		
sumum	a-certain		
swa	so		
swa	as		
sweartra	darkness		
symle	forever		
talade	numbered		

4.5 Homiletic Fragment II

Text

	Ænglisc	Literal	English

1	*Gefeoh nu on ferðe*
	    ond to frofre geþeoh
		Rejoice now in spirit
		    and in satisfaction thrive
			Rejoice now in spirit
			    and thrive in satisfaction

2	*dryhtne þinum,*
	    ond þinne dom arær,
		the Lord yours,
		    and your glory raise up,
			of your Lord,
			    and raise up in glory,

3	*heald hordlocan,*
	    hyge fæste bind
		hold hoard-lock,
		    mind fasten bind
			hold the hoard-lock,
			    bind the mind fast

4	*mid modsefan.*
	    Monig biþ uncuþ
		with spirit.
		    Many be unknowing
			with spirit.
			    Many are unknowing

5	*treowgeþofta,*
	    teorað hwilum,
		trusted-friends,
		    fail sometimes,
			trusted friends,
			    sometimes they fail,

6	*waciaþ wordbeot;*
	    swa þeos woruld fareð,
		awaken promise;
		    so this world fares,
			to awaken their word vows,
			    and so fares the world,

7	*scurum scyndeð*
	    ond gesceap dreogeð.
		storms surged
		    and creation enduring.
			in storms surged
			    and enduring creation.

8	*An is geleafa,*
	    an lifgende,
		One is faith,
		    one living,
			Faith is one,
			    The living are one,

9	*an is fulwiht,*
	    an fæder ece,
		one is baptism,
		    one father everlasting,
			The baptism is one,
			    The everlasting father is one,

10	*an is folces fruma,*
	    se þas foldan gesceop,
		one is the people creator,
		    who this earth made,
			The origin of people is one,
			    who made this earth,

11	*duguðe ond dreamas.*
	    Dom siþþan weox,
		goods and joys.
		    Judgement afterwards waxed,
			its goods and joys.
			    Judgement waxed afterwards,

12	*þeah þeos læne gesceaft*
	    longe stode
		though this loaned world
		    for a long time stood
			though this loaned world
			    stood for a long time

13	*heolstre gehyded,*
	    helme ...edygled,
		dark concealed,
		    shield ...the country,
			concealed in the dark,
			    covered by a shield,

14	*biþeaht wel treowum,*
	    þystre oferfæðmed,
		surrounded well trees,
		    darkness covered,
			surrounded well by trees,
			    covered with darkness,

15	*siþþan geong aweox*	afterwards the young grow	afterwards the youth grow

16	*mægeð modhwatu*
	    mid moncynne;
		maiden strong souled
		    among mankind;
			a maiden strong-souled
			    among mankind

17	*ðær gelicade*
	    þa... ...op
		there likened
		    then... ...out of
			there likened
			    then... ...out of

18	*in þam hordfate,*
	    halgan gæste,
		in the vessel,
		    holy ghost,
			in the vessel,
			    the holy spirit,

19	*beorht on br...*
	    ...e scan,
		bright in br...
		    ...e shining,
			bright in ...
			    … shining,

20	*se wæs ordfruma*
	    ealles leohtes.
		he was creator
		    every light.
			he was the creator
			    of all light

Word List

Ænglisc	English	Ænglisc	English
an	one	*hwilum*	sometimes
aræer	raise up	*hyge*	mind
aweox	grow	*in*	in
beorht	bright	*is*	is
bind	bind	*læne*	loaned
biþ	be	*leohtes*	light
biþeaht	surrounded	*lifgende*	living
br	br	*longe*	for a long time
ðæer	there	*mæged*	maiden
dom	glory	*mid*	among
dom	judgement	*mid*	with
dreamas	joys	*modhwatu*	strong souled
dreogeð	enduring	*modsefan*	spirit
dryhtne	the Lord	*moncynne*	mankind
duguðe	goods	*monig*	many
e	e	*nu*	now
ealles	every	*oferfæðmed*	covered
ece	everlasting	*on*	in
edygled	the country	*ond*	and
fæder	father	*op*	out of
fæste	fasten	*ordfruma*	creator
fareð	fares	*scan*	shining
ferðe	spirit	*scurum*	storms
folces	the people	*scyndeð*	surged
foldan	earth	*se*	he
frofre	satisfaction	*se*	who
fruma	creator	*siþþan*	afterwards
fulwiht	baptism	*stode*	stood
gæste	ghost	*swa*	so
gefeoh	rejoice	*teorað*	fail
gehyded	concealed	*þa*	then
geleafa	faith	*þam*	the
gelicade	likened	*þas*	this
geong	the young	*þeah*	though
gesceaft	world	*þeos*	this
gesceap	creation	*þinne*	your
gesceop	made	*þinum*	yours
geþeoh	thrive	*þystre*	darkness
halgan	holy	*to*	in
heald	hold	*treowgeþofta*	trusted-friends
helme	shield	*treowum*	trees
heolstre	dark	*uncuþ*	unknowing
hordfate	vessel	*waciaþ*	awaken
hordlocan	hoard-lock	*wæs*	was

Ænglisc	English
wel	well
weox	waxed
wordbeot	word-vows
woruld	world

4.6 Wulf and Eadwacer

Text

Ænglisc	Literal	English

1   *Leodum is minum*
     swylce him mon lac gife;
	The people that are mine
	     such is he one offered a gift;
		To my people
		     as if someone gave them a gift;

2   *willað hy hine aþecgan,*
     gif he on þreat cymeð.
	will they him to kill,
	     if he in a troop arrives.
		they want to kill him,
		     if he arrives in a troop.

3 *Ungelic is us.*	Unlike it is to us.	It is different for us.

4   *Wulf is on iege,*
     ic on oþerre.
	Wulf is on island,
	     I on another.
		Wulf is on an island,
		     and I am on another.

5   *Fæst is þæt eglond,*
     fenne biworpen.
	Fastened is that island,
	     by fens surrounded.
		Secured is that island,
		     surrounded by fens.

6   *Sindon wælreowe*
     weras þær on ige;
	They are bloodthirsty
	     men there on the island;
		They are bloodthirsty
		     the men there on the island;

7   *willað hy hine aþecgan,*
     gif he on þreat cymeð.
	will they him to kill,
	     if he in a troop arrives.
		they want to kill him,
		     if he arrives in a troop.

8 *Ungelice is us.*	Unlike it is to us.	It is different for us.

9   *Wulfes ic mines widlastum*
 	
     wenum dogode;
	To Wulf I mine far-wandering
	
	     hopes for days;
		To my Wulf I with far-wandering
		     hopes for days;

10   *þonne hit wæs renig weder*
     ond ic reotugu sæt,
	whenever it was rainy weather
	     and I mournfully sat,
		whenever it was rainy weather
		     and I sat mournfully,

11   *þonne mec se beaducafa*
     bogum bilegde,
	whenever I the brave-warrior's
	     arms covered,
		whenever the brave warrior's
		     arms covered me,

12   *wæs me wyn to þon,*
     wæs me hwæþre eac lað.
	was to me delight to that,
	     was to me however also loathsome.
		that was a delight to me,
		     but was also painful.

13   *Wulf, min Wulf,*
     wena me þine
	Wulf, my Wulf,
	     hopes mine to you
		Wulf, my Wulf,
		     my hopes for you

14   *seoce gedydon,*
     þine seldcymas,
	a sickness did,
	     your seldom-coming,
		have caused a sickness,
		     your infrequent visits,

15   *murnende mod,*
     nales meteliste.
	mournful mood,
	     never food-lacking.
		a mournful spirit,
		     never lacking in food.

16   *Gehyrest þu, Eadwacer?*
     Uncerne earne hwelp
	Hear you, Eadwacer?
	     Ours somewhere a cub
		Do you hear, Eadwacer?
		     Somewhere our cub

17 *bireð Wulf to wuda.*	bears Wulf to the woods.	is carried by a wolf to the woods

18   *þæt mon eaþe tosliteð*
     þætte næfre gesomnad wæs,
	that one easily tears-apart
	     that never together was,
		that is easily torn apart
		     by that which was never together,

19 *uncer giedd geador.*	our poem together.	our poem together.

Word List

Ænglisc	English	*Ænglisc*	English
aþecgan	to kill	*minum*	mine
beaducafa	brave-warrior's	*mod*	mood
bilegde	covered	*mon*	one
bireð	bears	*murnende*	mournful
biworpen	surrounded	*næfre*	never
bogum	arms	*nales*	never
cymeð	arrives	*on*	in
dogode	for days	*on*	on
eac	also	*ond*	and
eadwacer	Eadwacer (a name)	*oþerre*	another
earne	somewhere	*renig*	rainy
eaþe	easily	*reotugu*	mournfully
eglond	island	*sæt*	sat
fæst	fastened	*se*	the
fenne	by fens	*seldcymas*	seldom-coming
geador	together	*seoce*	a sickness
gedydon	did	*sindon*	they are
gehyrest	hear	*swylce*	such
gesomnad	together	*þær*	there
giedd	poem	*þæt*	that
gif	if	*þætte*	that
gife	a gift	*þine*	to you
he	he	*þine*	your
him	is he	*þon*	that
hine	him	*þonne*	whenever
hit	it	*þreat*	a troop
hwæþre	however	*þu*	you
hwelp	a cub	*to*	to
hy	they	*tosliteð*	tears-apart
ic	I	*uncer*	our
iege	island	*uncerne*	ours
ige	the island	*ungelic*	unlike
is	is	*ungelice*	unlike
is	it is	*us*	to us
is	that are	*wælreowe*	bloodthirsty
lac	offered	*wæs*	was
laþ	loathsome	*weder*	weather
leodum	the people	*wena*	hopes
me	mine	*wenum*	hopes
me	to me	*weras*	men
mec	I	*widlastum*	far-wandering
meteliste	food-lacking	*willað*	will
min	my	*wuda*	the woods
mines	mine	*wulf*	Wulf (a name)

Ænglisc	English
wulfes	to Wulf (a name)
wyn	delight

5 Word List (Ænglisc to English)

Ænglisc	English	*Ænglisc*	English
		and	and
		andan	injury
		anes	a
		angolsexna	of the Anglo-Saxons

A, a

Ænglisc	English
a	a, all, always, ever, from
ab	from, from (Latin)
abbot	abbot
abolescit	fades-away (Latin)
abscondita	hidden (Latin), was hidden
ac	but, nevertheless
acænned	brought-forth
ace	grow, grows
acemannesceastre	Akeman's Town
acenned	born
acolað	grows-cold
aðas	oaths
Aðelwold	Æthelwold (a name)
adlegan	sick-person
adwæsce	quenched
aðystrað	grows-dark
aeðða	or
aelda	elders'
aerist	first
aeternus	eternal (Latin)
afera	heir-of
agælde	delaying
agangen	going
age	own
ahangen	hanged
ahengon	hung up
aidan	Aidan
alaðaþ	becomes-loathed
allmectig	almighty
almum	nurturing (Latin)
alswa	as
alta	heights
alysde	released
amen	amen
amor	love (Latin)
an	a, on, one
ana	alone
anbre	bucket

Ænglisc	English
and	and
andan	injury
anes	a
angolsexna	of the Anglo-Saxons
animæ	souls (Latin)
anum	one
aquilone	the north (Latin)
arær	raise up
aræred	raise
ardor	heat (Latin)
arfesta	merciful
asolað	grows-dirty
astelidæ	established
aþecgan	to kill
attorlaþe	cock's spur grass
auctor	author (Latin)
aurnen	passed
austro	the south (Latin)
awage	away
aweox	grow
awrat	wrote

Æ, æ

Ænglisc	English
æce	eternal
æcum	eternal
æðela	noble
æðele	nobility, noble
æðelinges	noble's
æðelredes	Æthelred's
æðelum	noble
æðelwold	Aethelwold
æfter	after, after
æghwæt	everything
æhtum	possessions
ælcre	each
ælfheres	Ælfhere's
Ælfrices	Ælfric's (a name)
ælmessan	alms
ælmihtig	almighty
æminde	forgetfulness
æne	at once

Ænglisc	English	*Ænglisc*	English
Ænglisc	English, any	*betest*	the best
ænyg	any	*Bethlem*	Bethlehem
ær	before, before, first	*bewerode*	defended
ærest	first	*bi*	about
æror	before	*biblos*	the book (Latin)
æt	at, from me	*bið*	be, being
æterna	eternal (Latin)	*biddan*	ask
æþele	a noble	*bidde*	ask, pray
æþelne	noble, nobler	*bide*	pray
æþelre	noble	*bideð*	awaits
æþelum	noble	*bilegde*	covered
Æþlmær	Æthelmaer (a name)	*bind*	bind
		binnan	within
		bireð	bears
		biscop	bishop
		bitera	bitter

B, b

Ænglisc	English	*Ænglisc*	English
baðan	Bath	*biþ*	be
bæðleem	Bethlehem	*biþeaht*	surrounded
bær	bore	*biworpen*	surrounded
bæteran	better	*blac*	bright
barnum	children	*blæd*	glory
be	about	*bliðemod*	blithe-mood
beadowræda	battle bandage	*bliðmod*	blithe-minded
beaducafa	brave-warrior's	*blis*	rejoicing
bealuleas	the innocent	*blode*	bloodied
bearn	children, son	*boca*	of books
bearna	children's	*bocera*	writer of books
bearnum	children, son	*bodade*	heralded
beatus	blessed (Latin)	*boethia*	Boethius
becom	came	*bogum*	arms
beda	Bede	*boisil*	Boisil
befæste	entrusted	*bona*	good (Latin)
begytan	obtain	*bonus*	a good
belegde	covered	*br*	br
benne	the wound, this wound	*brada*	broad
beo	be	*breðel*	brittle
beoð	shall be	*bremes*	celebrated
beorht	bright	*breoma*	celebrated
beorhte	bright	*breome*	famous
beorn	nobleman	*breotenrice*	Britain-kingdom
beornas	children-of-men	*bretene*	Britain
beoþ	be	*brimstream*	ocean-stream
bereafod	bereft	*britnian*	dispense
berhge	hill	*britnode*	bestowed
beroþor	brother	*broþer*	brother
bestemed	wet		

Ænglisc	English	Ænglisc	English
brymmas	waves	col	coal
brytnodon	bestowed	colian	became-cold
bryttum	the Britons	com	came
bufan	above	coman	came
burch	city	consolde	comfrey
Burga	boroughs	constantinus	Constantinus
burgenda	of the Burgundians	corðre	assembly
burgum	cities	cosmi	of the world (Latin)
burh	town	cosmo	the world
burnon	burn	costunga	temptation
burston	burst	cræftig	skilful
buruh	town	Crist	Christ, Christ (a name)
butan	except, without	criste	Christ, Christ (a name)
buton	except	cristes	Christ's
byð	be	crop	sprout
byfigynde	trembling	crucem	the cross
byre	his child	Crux	the cross, the cross (Latin)
byri	city	cudberch	Cuthbert
byrig	town	cudberte	Cuthbert
byrnan.	armour	cum	with (Latin)
byrnende	burning	cunne	know
byscop	a bishop	cuþe	be able to

C, c

Ænglisc	English
caelorum	of heaven (Latin)
cassuc	cassock
casta	chaste
cealde	cold
ceap	property
ceapa	cattle
cennan	bear
Christi	of Christ
christum	Christ (Latin)
christus	Christ (Latin)
cigað	call
clænan	clean
clæne	chaste, clean
clara	clear (Latin)
clea	claw
clemens	clement (Latin)
clene	clean
clinge	shrink
cnut	Canute
cnyssan	drive

Ænglisc	English
cwæð	saying
cweð	say
cweðan	speak
cweðe	say
cwet	saying
cweþ	say
cweþe	say
Cwyð	say
cyme	come
cymeð	arrives
cyning	king, king, king
cyninga	kings
cyningc	king of
cyninge	king
cyninges	king, king's
cyst	choice

D, d

Ænglisc	English
dæd	deed, deed

Ænglisc	English
dæda	deeds
dædfruma	deed-doer
dædum	deeds
dæg	day, the day
dæge	day
Dæne	Danes
dagas	days
dalum	dales
de	of (Latin)
deað	death
deaðdege	death-day
deaþe	death
demed	deemed
dena	the Danes
deoðdaege	death-day
deope	deep
deor	beasts
deora	deer
Deoraby	Derby
deore	dear, the dear
derian	harm
deus	god (Latin)
dile	dill
dinamis	powerful (Latin)
dionisius	Dionisius
diopian	deepen
do	do
docce	sorrel
doemed	deemed
doemid	deemed
dogode	for days
dolh	the pain
dom	glory, judgement
doma	deeming
domę	glory
domes	judgement
domfæstne	judgement-firm
Dor	The Dore
dreamas	joys
dreame	rejoicing
dreogeð	enduring
drihnes	Lord's
drihten	lord, the Lord
drihtne	lord
dryctin	lord

Ænglisc	English
dryhten	the-lord
dryhtne	the Lord, the-lord
duguðe	goods, virtue
dweores	the dwarf's
dweorh	a dwarf
dydon	doing
dydon.	did
dyre	dear
dyrre	dare

Ð, ð

Ænglisc	English
ða	that, the, then
ðæm	the, the
ðær	that, there
ðære	there
ðæt	that
ðam	that, the
ðe	as, of, that, the, to-thee, which, who
ðeah	yet
ðearf	needs
ðegen	thane
ðem	these, they
ðence	intent
ðene	the
ðeoda	nations
ðeodric	Theodric
ðeos	this
ðer	there
ðere	this
ðes	these, this
ði	the
ðis	this
ðohte	thought
ðon	than
ðonne	then, when
ðonosnottorra	thought-wiser
ðreat	crowd
ðu	you
ðurh	through
ðus	thus
ðusend	thousand

Ænglisc	English	Ænglisc	English
		ec	other
		ece	eternal, everlasting
		eci	eternal

E, e

Ænglisc	English	Ænglisc	English
e	e	eðel	country
ea	river	eðle	homeland
eac	also, too	edygled	the country
eadberch	Eadbert	efne	even
eadelenan	Blessed-Helen (a name)	eft	after, afterwards, again
eadfrið	Eadfrid	efter	after
eadgan	blessed	eglond	island
eadgar	Edgar	elehtre	lupine
eadig	blessed	ellen	elder
eadige	blessed	ellenrof	courageous
Eadmund	Eadmund, Edmund	elles	anything-else
eadmundes	Edmund's	encratea	power-inside
eadwacer	Eadwacer (a name)	end	and
eadward	Edward	ende	end
eadwarde	Edward	engla	Engla, English
Eadweardes	Edward	englas	angels
eafora	descendants	engle	Angli
eagan	eyes	englum	the Angles
eal	all	enne	a
ealaþ	ale	eoforþrote	carline thistle
ealdan	old	eolone	elecampane
ealdelm	Aldhelm	eom	am
ealdor	lord	eonene	pass
eall	all	eorðan	earth, elders', the earth
ealle	all	eorðe	earth
ealles	all, every	eorle	earl
eallum	all	eorþan	earth, the earth
ealne	all	eorþe	earth
ealneg	always	eow	you
ealra	all	eowberge	yew berry
eardast	dwell	ermig	in pain
eardiæð	inhabited	est	is, is (Latin)
eardwica	dwelling place	et	and, and (Latin), on
eare	ear, ears	eþeles	homeland
earne	somewhere	etiam	also (Latin)
earnes	eagle's, the eagle's	euthenia	prosperity
earnian	earning		
earnunga	earning		
eart	be		

F, f

Ænglisc	English	Ænglisc	English
east	east		
eaþe	easily	factor	maker (Latin)
eaxelum	shoulders		

Ænglisc	English	*Ænglisc*	English
fæder	father	*fone*	take
fæger	fair	*for*	because, because-of, for
fægere	beautifully, good		
fæst	fastened	*forð*	forth
fæste	fasten	*fore*	for
fah	hostile	*forealdað*	grows-old
fareð	fares	*foręldit*	delays
Farones	Pharoah's	*forhelan*	conceal, hidden
feðewigges	foot-battle	*forholen*	hidden
felterre	felterry	*forlet;*	released
fenminte	fen mint	*fornam*	swept-away
fenne	by fens	*forstolen*	stolen
feogan	hating	*fortis*	strength (Latin)
feoh	cattle	*forweorp*	throw
feola	many	*fot*	foot
feologan	become fallow	*frætewum*	ornaments
feondscipe	enmity	*fram*	from
feondum.	his enemies	*frea*	lord
feore	life	*frean*	lord
feorhhord	soul-hoard	*fremaþ*	acts
ferðe	spirit	*freodom*	freedom
fere	drive	*freolic*	freely
feredon	carried	*freolice*	freely, splendid
fet	foot	*frequenter*	frequently (Latin)
feta	take	*friclo*	aid
fiað	let it be so	*frigesscit*	grows-cold (Latin)
fife	five	*friþes*	peace
fifela	a monster's	*froda*	wise
filius	son (Latin)	*frofre*	satisfaction
find	find	*from*	away
findan	find	*fruma*	creator
findanne	find	*fugle*	bird
findeð	finds	*fuit*	he was (Latin)
finit	the end	*fultum*	comfort
firene	sin	*fultumes*	eagerly
firum	for-men	*fulwiht*	baptism
fisca	fish	*funde*	found
fleogan	fly	*fundian*	forwards
floda	flood	*fylgan*	pursued
fo	receive, take	*fylste*	support
folc	folk	*fyrde*	army
folca	folk		
folces	the people		
foldan	earth, lands		
foldu	lands		

G, g

Ænglisc	English
ga	let

Ænglisc	English	Ænglisc	English
gæste	ghost	*gehwilce*	every
gahwem	undertaking	*gehwilces*	matters
galdor	chant	*gehwylcre*	works
gangan	walking	*gehyded*	concealed
garmund	Garmund (a name)	*gehyrest*	hear
gast	spirit	*gelæde*	leads
gastae	spirit, spirit	*gelamp*	happened
gaste	spirit	*geleafa*	faith
ge	you	*gelicade*	likened
geador	together	*gelifeð*	trusts
geændade	interceded	*gemæne*	universal
gealdor	chant	*gemærsod*	made famous, made-famous
geanoðe	meeting	*gemearcian*	to-mark
geapneb	cleverly-woven	*gemetað*	meet with
gearo	ready	*gemiltsað*	have mercy
geatwum	trappings	*gemind*	thoughts
gebegde	bowed	*gemindige*	mindful
gebide	abide, look	*gemonge*	together
geboren	born	*gemynde*	mindful
gebroþor	brethren	*gemyndi*	mindful
gebyrd	birth	*gen*	yet
gebyrdtide	the-birth	*genam*	seized, taken
gecheðe	youth	*genom*	took
gecwæð	said	*Geo*	once
gecyðed	well-known	*geomres*	mournful
gecyrre	turn	*geond*	around, over
geðenceð.	considers	*geong*	the young
gedidon	did	*geonges*	youth's
gedige	prosper	*georne*	eagerly
gedo	do	*geornor*	gladly
gedydon	did	*gerimes*	number, numbered
geeode	conquered	*gesæd*	spoken
gefeoh	rejoice	*gesælða*	of peace
geferes	associates	*gesceaft*	world
gefrege	noted	*gesceap*	creation
gefremede	prevail	*gesceop*	created, made
gefremian	accomplish	*gescyred*	alloted
gegaderod	gathered	*gesette*	composed
gegirwan	adorned	*gesomnad*	together
gehalgod	consecrated	*gestaðolad*	founded
gehicgenne	think	*geswicað*	abandon
gehided.	hidden	*get*	agreed
gehwæs	each	*geteled*	reckoned
gehwam	every	*geþancie*	thank
gehwilc	each	*geþeoh*	thrive

Ænglisc	English	Ænglisc	English
geþohte	thought	*hæncgest*	horse
geþungen	gracefully	*hærran*	lord
getwæmde	separate	*hæþenra*	heathen
geunne	grant	*hafa*	have
gewæxen	grown	*hafað*	has
geweald	domain	*hagenan*	Hagen's
geweorðad	give worthiness to	*hagestealde*	young and brave
geweorðod	adorned	*haleg*	holy
geweornie	wither away	*halewæge*	the hallows
gewexen	grown	*halgad*	hallowed
geworden	agreed, became	*halgan*	holy, holy one
gewritu	writings	*halgungboc*	holy-book
gewurðað	being	*halig*	holy
gewurþe	become	*haligan*	holy
giedd	poem	*haligne*	holy
gief	give	*ham*	home
gif	if	*haman*	horse-collar
gife	a gift	*hand*	hand
gihuaes	each	*handa*	hand, hands
gioce	support	*handwurmes*	hand-worm's
gleaw	learned	*hare*	grey
gleawra	skilful	*harolde*	Harold
god	good	*hat*	heat
godaes	good	*hattæ*	is named
gode	god	*hatte*	named
godes	God-heathen's, God's, good, wellbeing	*hauest*	have
God's	God's	*he*	he, it
golde	gold	*heaðuwerigan*	battle-weary
greot	earth	*heafde*	face
gripe	gripped	*heafud*	head
guðbilla	battle-bill	*heahþungenum*	high-ranking
gyddode	spoke	*heald*	hold
gyf	if	*healde*	hold
gyfe	gave	*healfe*	half
		heap	pile
		heard	bitter

H, h

Ænglisc	English	Ænglisc	English
habbanne	have	*heben*	heaven
habben	have	*hefaenricaes*	heaven-kingdom's
hæfde	had	*hellfirena*	hell-fire-like
hæfteclommum	binding-chains	*helme*	shield
hæleða	saviour	*helpe*	help
hæligwæter	holy water	*helpend*	help
hælon	covering, hit	*helpes*	for help
		heo	she
		heofon	heaven

Ænglisc	English	*Ænglisc*	English
heofonrices	heaven-kingdom's	*hweorfað*	turn
heofonum	heaven	*hwet*	what-of
heolstre	dark	*hwilcne*	which
heom	with them	*hwilum*	sometimes
heonengange	from-here-goes	*hwit*	white
heonon	from-here	*Hwitanwyllesgeat*	Whitwell Gap
heortan	heart	*hwylce*	such
heorþe	hearth	*hy*	he, they
her	here	*hyge*	mind, soul
hergan	honour	*hyra*	their
herigean	honour	*hyrde*	heard, obeyed
herod	Herod (a name)	*hyrdes*	keeper
het	commanded, ordered	*hyrdon*	obeyed
hi	it, the, they	*hys*	his
hie	he	*hyt*	it
hilde	battle		
hildefrofre	weapon		
him	he, him, his, is he, it, the, to-him		

I, i

Ænglisc	English	*Ænglisc*	English
hine	he, him	*iamiamque*	right now (Latin)
hiniongae	from-here-goes	*ic*	I
hinionge	from-here-goes	*iege*	island
hire	these	*igbuend*	islanders
his	he, his	*ige*	the island
hit	he, it, of it	*III*	three-times
hlaf	bread	*in*	in, into, the-chamber
hlaford	lord	*innan*	into, within
hleo	protecting	*inne*	in
ho	hang	*inswiden*	singed
holdlice	graciously, loyally	*inuenta*	found, found (Latin)
hoppettan	throb	*iohannes*	Iohannes
hordfate	vessel	*ipselos*	high (Latin)
hordlocan	hoard-lock	*is*	is, it is, that are
hrofe	a roof, a-roof	*Iudeas*	Judas
huaet	what-of	*iudex*	judge (Latin)
Humbra	Humber	*iulean*	reward
hun	hundred	*iustus*	just (Latin)
hund	hundred		
hupeban	hipbone		
huru	surely		
husa	houses		

K, k

Ænglisc	English	*Ænglisc*	English
hwa	who	*kingc*	the king
hwæt	hear, indeed, what, what-of	*kinge*	king
		kyn	kinds
hwæþre	however	*kyneþrymme*	royal-power
hwelp	a cub	*kyng*	king

Ænglisc	English	*Ænglisc*	English
kyningc	a king	*litel*	little
kynn	kin	*liþan*	journey
kystum	of virtues	*liþu*	limbs
		locian	to look
		lofe	love

L, l

Ænglisc	English	*Ænglisc*	English
labor	work	*longe*	for a long time
lac	offered	*losod*	lost
lace	offer	*loue*	love
lacnað	healed	*luce*	light (Latin)
ladigan	excuse	*lufianne*	love
læcedome	remedy	*lungre*	suddenly
læne	loaned	*lustum*	joyfully
læt	allow	*lux*	light (Latin)
laf	legacy	*lytle*	little
lafe	remain		
land	land		

M, m

Ænglisc	English
lande	land, of land
landes	Land
lange	long
lara	learning
lata	slack
laþ	loathsome
leaf	a leaf, leaf
lean	reward
leas	FALSE
leg	lays
legde	laid
legge	lay
leng	longer
leo	lion
leode	people
leodum	the people
leof	love
leoht	light
leohta	light
leohtes	light
lerde	learned
lesse	smaller
life	life
lifgende	living
Ligoraceaster	Leicester
lilie	lily
Lincylene	Lincoln
linsetcorn	linseed

Ænglisc	English
ma	greater, more
maðelode	spoke
madma	treasures
maðma	treasure
mæcgea	kinsmen
maecti	might
mædenman	maiden
mæg	kinsman, may, may be
mægeð	maiden
mægen	strengths
mægenum	power
mæra	famous
mære	distinguished, famous
mæst	most
magna	great (Latin)
malchus	Malchus
man	a man, man, one
manega	many
manegum	many
manna	men
mannes	man's, person's
marian	Mary
martimianus	Martimianus
marubie	marrabulum
maximianus	Maximianus
me	me, mine, on me, to me
meahte	might

Ænglisc	English	Ænglisc	English
mec	I	monig	many
mece	Sword	monige	many
mecum	sword	monnum	mankind
menn	man, men	moste	be able to
meotod	creator	motan	be allowed to
meotodes	the-measurer's	moten	may
meridie	the south	mundbora	guardian
merscmealwan	marshmallow	mundcræftas	protection-powers
meteliste	food-lacking	mundi	of the world (Latin), the world's (Latin)
metes	food		
metod	creator	mundum	the world (Latin)
metode	the-Creator, the-Creator	muneca	monk
		murnende	mournful
metudæs	the-measurer's	myrce	Mercia
miccli	much		
micel	great, many, much		
micelan	great		
miclum	great		

N, n

Ænglisc	English	Ænglisc	English
micro	little (Latin)	n	(name)
mid	among, with	næbbe	not-have
midd	the middle, with	næfre	never
middangeard	middle-earth	næglas	nails
middungeard	middle-earth	næni	none
mihta	might, mighty, powers	naenig	none
mihtan	might	nænige	none
mihte	might	næs	by-no-means
mihton	might	nales	never
mihtum	might	nalles	not at all
milde	merciful, mild	nama	name
min	my	naman	names
mine	of mind	nanuht	nothing
mines	mine, my	nat	not
minstre	ministers	nawiht	nothing
minum	mine	ne	do not, does not, neither, nor, not
mod	heart, mood		
modes	mind's	neah	nigh
modgeþanc	mind-plans	nearwum	captivity
modgidanc	mind-plans	nedfere	needed-journey
modhwatu	strong souled	neidfaerae	needed-journey
modsefan	spirit	nemnað	name
moldan	top-of-the-head	nemnaþ	name
mon	one, someone	nenig	none
moncynnæs	mankind's	nenne	any
moncynne	mankind	nergend	saviour
moncynnes	mankind's	niða	murmuring
monia	many	niðhades	Nithad's

79

Ænglisc	English	*Ænglisc*	English
niðweorca	conflict	*oftor*	often
nigon	nine	*oliccan*	praise
nihgan	next	*omnes*	all (Latin)
nihtum	nights	*omnia*	everything (Latin)
nim	take	*on*	about, in, of, on, over
niman	take	*onbere*	withers
nioþo	from below	*ond*	and
niþer	downwards	*onette*	hasten
niþþa	men	*onfo*	receive
nitor	shining (Latin)	*ongalan*	recite
noma	the name	*ongunn*	undertake
non	not (Latin)	*ongunnan*	began
norð	north	*ongynnað*	assail
Norðmannum	Northmen	*onsended*	sent
north	north	*onsendon*	to send
Nu	now	*onstealde*	established
nusquam	never (Latin)	*op*	out of
nyde	subjected	*or*	origin
		orbem	the world (Latin)
		ordfruma	creator
		oretmægcum	warriors
		orf	cattle

O, o

Ænglisc	English
obtenebrescit	grows-dark (Latin)
occidente	the west, the west (Latin)
oððe	or
oðehtian	disposess
oðfeorrganne	drive-away
oðfergean	drive-away
oðferie	drive-off
oðhealde	keep-away
oðlædanne	lead-off
oðlæde	lead-off
oðre	another
oðres	other
oðþæt	until
oðwyrceanne	destroy
of	from, of
ofer	over
ofercom	overcame
oferfæðmed	covered
oferweorp	throw down
ofgeot	soak
oflætan	wafer, wafers
ofrað	offertory
oft	often

Ænglisc	English
oriente	the east, the east (Latin)
osuualdes	Oswald's
oþ	until
oþer	other
oþerre	another
oþþe	or

P, p

Ænglisc	English
pacis	of peace (Latin)
partu	birth
pentecostenes	Pentecost
per	by
perhennem	perpetual
pleno	full (Latin)
polleie	pennyroyal
polorum	of the poles (Latin)
pondus	weight (Latin)
ponus	work (Latin)
preosta	priests

Ænglisc	English
Q, q	
que	which (Latin)
quem	who (Latin)
qui	who (Latin)
R, r	
ræda	counsel
rædfæst	righteous
rædfest	sound
reaf	vestment
recon	ready
redemptor	redeemer (Latin)
reducað	is led (Latin)
reducant	led
reducat	is led (Latin), led
regem	the king (Latin)
regentem	ruling (Latin)
regit	rules (Latin)
regna	kingdom (Latin)
reliquia	relics
renig	rainy
reotugu	mournfully
restað	rest
reþehygdig	right-thinking
rhyta	rights
rice	kingdom
ricne	a-powerful
rimde	the host
rime	counted
rimes	counted
Rod	cross
rode	cross
rodores	the heavens
rogo	pray (Latin)
rume	roomy
rumre	wide
ryhte	properly
S, s	
sæt	sat

Ænglisc	English
saga	tell
salus	salvation (Latin)
sanctæ	holy (Latin)
sancte	saint
sancti	the saints (Latin)
sanctus	saintly
saule	soul
sawla	souls
sawle	soul
scadeþ	borders
scan	shining
sceal	shall, should
scealt	shall
sceððan	harm
sceop	created, poet
scepen	shaper
scerne	dung
scine	shines
scolde	should
scop	created
scottum	the Scots
screoda	numbered
scring	shrivel
sculon	shall-we
scurum	storms
scylun	shall-we
scyndeð	surged
scyppend	shaper
se	he, so, the, who
searohæbbendra	armoured
secgað	say
secgan	tell, told
secge	says
sedentem	sitting on (Latin)
seggeð	say
sel	better
selast	excellence
seldcymas	seldom-coming
self	himself
selfum	himself
sende	sent
senescunt	grows-old (Latin)
sensu	sense (Latin)
seo	be, it, the
seoce	a sickness

Ænglisc	English	*Ænglisc*	English
seofon	seven	*suð*	south
serafion	Serafion	*sue*	as
sexum	the Saxons	*summi*	highest (Latin)
siae	to-be	*summo*	highest (Latin)
sibbe	joys	*summus*	highest (Latin)
siblufan	love	*sumum*	a-certain
sie	to-be	*sunt*	they, they-are (Latin)
siex	six	*sunu*	son
sigað	sink	*supplex*	supplicant (Latin)
sige	victory	*swa*	as, so, thus
sigewif	victorious-women	*sweartra*	darkness
sigisiþa	successful	*swegles*	heaven's
sigora	victories	*sweoran*	neck
simle	ever	*sweostar*	sister
sinc	riches	*swiðe*	exceedingly
sindon	they are	*swiðre*	right
sing	sing	*swirman*	swarming
singalan	continuously	*swiþran*	right
singan	sing	*swor*	swore
sinum	his	*swylce*	likewise, such, such as
siþþan	afterwards, thenceforth	*swyltit*	dies
siþum	afterwards	*sy*	be, is, to-be
sitte	sit	*syððan*	since
snotera	wiser	*syle*	give
Snotingaham	Nottingham	*sylfan*	his-self
soð	truly	*sylfum*	himself
soðfæst	truth-firm	*syllan*	give
soðfæsta	truth-fastened	*symle*	always, forever
soðfæstan	truth-fastened	*synna*	sin
soðum	TRUE	*syre*	rotten
sona	as soon, at once, soon		
soþfæste	righteous	**T, t**	
squalescit	grows-dirty (Latin)		
stæl	place of	*talade*	numbered
stanas	stones	*teage*	ties
standeð	stands	*tearige*	teary
stanfate	jewelled-sheath	*tenet*	holds (Latin)
Stanford	Stamford	*teode*	titled
steppa	steps	*teorað*	fail
stille	quietly	*throno*	thrones
stode	stood	*thronum*	the throne
stolenne	stolen	*tiadæ*	titled
streawbergean	strawberry	*tid*	a time, time
stronge	strong	*tiid*	time

Ænglisc	English	Ænglisc	English
til	for	*þeodne*	the prince
timbrien	build	*þeos*	this
tireadge	glorious	*þer*	there
to	for, forth, go to, in, to	*þet*	that
torhte	bright	*þi*	therefore
toscufeð	do-away	*þin*	your
tosliteð	tears-apart	*þine*	to you, your
treowe	faith	*þinga*	thing
treowgeþofta	trusted-friends	*þingian*	intercede
treowum	trees	*þinne*	your
tun	dwelling	*þinre*	your, yours
tungan	tongue	*þinum*	your, yours
twentig	twenty	*þis*	it, this
tyn	ten	*þon*	from there, that, then
		þoncsnotturra	thought-wiser
		þone	the, then, those

Þ, þ

Ænglisc	English	Ænglisc	English
þa	as, being, that, the, then, then, when	*þonne*	from there, from-there, than, then, there, those, when, whenever, whereby
þæm	that, the, they	*þrage*	for a time, for-a-time
þæne	the	*þreat*	a troop
þænne	then	*þriwa*	three times, three-times
þær	there		
þære	to the	*þry*	three
þæs	because, of-that, so, that, the, this	*þrym*	three
		þrymcyningc	the ruling king
þæt	that, the	*þu*	you
þætte	that	*þureð*	Thureth
þam	that, that, the, the, them	*þurh*	by, for the sake of, sake-of, through
þan	than, the	*þus*	thus
þance	thank	*þy*	by this
þances	thought	*þyos*	this
þarf	needs	*þystel*	thistle
þas	these, this	*þystre*	darkness
þe	any, for you, it, that, the, then, though, which, you		

U, u

Ænglisc	English	Ænglisc	English
þeah	nevertheless, though	*uard*	ward
þearf	necessary, needs	*uerc*	work-of
þence	intend, think	*ueþer*	wing
þenden	so long as	*uirginem*	the virgin (Latin)
þeoda	nations	*uirginis*	maiden (Latin)
þeoden	lord, the-lord	*uirtute*	virtue (Latin)
þeodkyninges	great-king		

Ænglisc	English	Ænglisc	English
uiuendo	living (Latin)	we	we
unarimeda	unnumbered	wealdan	rule over
uncer	our	wealdend	ruler
uncerne	ours	weallendan	welling
uncuþ	unknowing	weard	keep, ward
under	under	weder	weather
ungelic	unlike	wel	well
ungelice	unlike	welan	wealth
ungerim	innumerable	welandes	Weland's
unica	one (Latin)	wena	hopes
unmægas	unrelated	wenchichenne	little wen
unscende	blameless	wendest	expected
uoca	call (Latin)	wene	think
uoce	voice (Latin)	wenne	wen
uoluntate	will (Latin)	wenum	hopes
urne	our	weolan	wealth
us	to us, upon us, us	weold	ruling
userne	ours	weoldon	ruled
usic	us	weor	the Wear
ussum	us	weorc	work-of
ut	out	weorcum	work
uton	let us	weorðae	of-worth
uuldurfadur	glory-father	weorðmynda	worth-minded
uundra	wonder	weorne	evaporate
		weornie	waste-away
		weornige	waste-away
		weorþe	of-worth
		weorþscipe	worthship
		weorudes	troops
		weox	waxed
		wer	man
		wera	man, of man
		weras	men
		wereð	protects
		wereda	army
		wermod	wormwood
		wes	was
		west	west
		weter	water
		wið	against
		widan	wide
		wiððon	afterwards
		wide	wide, widely
		widia	Widia
		widian	to Widia

V, v

Ænglisc	English
vii	seven

W, w

Ænglisc	English
waciaþ	awaken
wælreowe	bloodthirsty
wæra	keeping
wæran	were
wære	were
wæs	to be, was
wæterælfadle	water elf disease
wætre	water
waldend	ruler
waldere	Waldere
walum	the Welsh
wat	know
waxsian	grow

Ænglisc	English	*Ænglisc*	English
widlastum	far-wandering	*wundorlicne*	wondrous
wiga	warrior	*wundra*	wonder
wiggendra	warriors	*wundrum*	wondrous, wondrously
wiht	creature	*wuniad*	live
wihta	beings	*wunian*	dwelling
wihte	anything	*wunode*	dwelt
wilda	wild	*wurðe*	worth
wilde	wild	*wurðmynt*	honour
wile	willing	*wurþe*	become
willa	will	*wycum*	dwellings
willað	will	*wyle*	wishes
wine	friend	*wyn*	delight
wintergeteles	winters-numbered	*wynstre*	left
wintra	winters	*wyrcean*	created
wiorðe.	of-worth	*wyrde*	destroyed
wiorðeð	will-be	*wyrðe*	become
witanne	protect	*wyrican*	made
wiurðit	will-be	*wyrrestan*	worst
wlance	the proud	*wyrstan*	worst
wlite	beauty	*wyrþe*	become
wolues	the wolf's	*wyrþeþ*	will-be
wonne	dark		
word	word		
wordbeot	word-vows		
worde	word		
wordum	words		
woruld	world		
worulda	the world		
worulde	the-world		
woruldrice	world-kingdom		
wræclastum	outcast		
wraþe	wrathfully		
writ	writings		
writan	write		
wuda	the woods		
wudafæstern	wood-fastened		
wudu	wood		
wuldor	glory		
wuldorfæder	glory-father		
wuldres	glory, wondrous		
wulf	Wulf (a name)		
wulfes	to Wulf (a name)		
wunað	dwell		
wund	wound		
wunde	wounds		

X, x

Ænglisc	English
xx	twenty
xxiiii	twenty four
xxviii	twenty-eight
xxx	thirty

Y, y

Ænglisc	English
yðum	waves
yfel	badly
yfeles	evil
yfla	evil
yflaes	evil
yfles	evil
ymbclyppað	embraced
ymbe	a swarm of bees
ymbeornad	beholds
ymbhycgenne	about-think
ymbhycggannae	about-think
ymbutan	about
yþ	wave

6 Word List (English to Ænglisc)

English	Ænglisc

A, a

English	Ænglisc
a	a, an, anes, enne
a bishop	byscop
a cub	hwelp
a dwarf	dweorh
a gift	gife
a good	bonus
a king	kyningc
a leaf	leaf
a man	man
a monster's	fifela
a noble	æþele
a roof	hrofe
a sickness	seoce
a swarm of bees	ymbe
a time	tid
a troop	þreat
abandon	geswicað
abbot	abbot
abide	gebide
about	be, bi, on, ymbutan
about-think	ymbhycgenne, ymbhycggannae
above	bufan
accomplish	gefremian
a-certain	sumum
acts	fremaþ
adorned	gegirwan, geweorðod
Aethelwold	æðelwold
after	æfter, aefter, eft, efter
afterwards	eft, siþþan, siþum, wiððon
again	eft
against	wið
agreed	get, geworden
aid	friclo
Aidan	aidan
Akeman's Town	acemannesceastre
Aldhelm	ealdelm
ale	ealaþ

English	Ænglisc
all	a, eal, eall, ealle, ealles, eallum, ealne, ealra
all (Latin)	omnes
alloted	gescyred
allow	læt
almighty	ælmihtig, allmectig
alms	ælmessan
alone	ana
also	eac
also (Latin)	etiam
always	a, ealneg, symle
am	eom
amen	amen
among	mid
and	and, end, et, ond
and (Latin)	et
angels	englas
Angli	engle
another	oðre, oþerre
any	ænyg, nenne, þe
anything	wihte
anything-else	elles
a-powerful	ricne
armour	byrnan.
armoured	searohæbbendra
arms	bogum
army	fyrde, wereda
a-roof	hrofe
around	geond
arrives	cymeð
as	alswa, ðe, sue, swa, þa
as soon	sona
ask	biddan, bidde
assail	ongynnað
assembly	corðre
associates	geferes
at	æt
at once	æne, sona
author (Latin)	auctor
awaits	bideð
awaken	waciaþ

English	Ænglisc	English	Ænglisc
away	awage, from	Bethlehem	bæðleem, Bethlem
		better	bæteran, sel
		bind	bind

Æ, æ

		binding-chains	hæfteclommum
		bird	fugle
Ælfhere's	ælfheres	birth	gebyrd, partu
Ælfric's (a name)	Ælfrices	bishop	biscop
Æthelmaer (a name)	Æþlmær	bitter	bitera, heard
Æthelred's	æðelredes	blameless	unscende
Æthelwold (a name)	Aðelwold	blessed	eadgan, eadig, eadige
		blessed (Latin)	beatus
		Blessed-Helen (a name)	eadelenan

B, b

		blithe-minded	bliðmod
		blithe-mood	bliðemod
badly	yfel	bloodied	blode
baptism	fulwiht	bloodthirsty	wælreowe
Bath	baðan	Boethius	boethia
battle	hilde	Boisil	boisil
battle bandage	beadowræda	borders	scadeþ
battle-bill	guðbilla	bore	bær
battle-weary	heaðuwerigan	born	acenned, geboren
be	beo, beoþ, bið, biþ, byð, eart, seo, sy	boroughs	Burga
be able to	cuþe, moste	bowed	gebegde
be allowed to	motan	br	br
bear	cennan	brave-warrior's	beaducafa
bears	bireð	bread	hlaf
beasts	deor	brethren	gebroþor
beautifully	fægere	bright	beorht, beorhte, blac, torhte
beauty	wlite		
became	geworden	Britain	bretene
became-cold	colian	Britain-kingdom	breotenrice
because	for, þæs	brittle	breðel
because-of	for	broad	brada
become	gewurþe, wurþe, wyrðe, wyrþe	brother	beroþor, broþer
		brought-forth	acænned
become fallow	feologan	bucket	anbre
becomes-loathed	alaðaþ	build	timbrien
Bede	beda	burn	burnon
before	ær, aer, æror	burning	byrnende
began	ongunnan	burst	burston
beholds	ymbeornad	but	ac
being	bið, gewurðað, þa	by	per, þurh
beings	wihta	by fens	fenne
bereft	bereafod	by this	þy
bestowed	britnode, brytnodon	by-no-means	næs

English	Ænglisc	English	Ænglisc

C, c

English	Ænglisc
call	cigað
call (Latin)	uoca
came	becom, com, coman
Canute	cnut
captivity	nearwum
carline thistle	eoforþrote
carried	feredon
cassock	cassuc
cattle	ceapa, feoh, orf
celebrated	bremes, breoma
chant	galdor, gealdor
chaste	casta, clæne
children	barnum, bearn, bearnum
children-of-men	beornas
children's	bearna
choice	cyst
Christ	Crist, criste
Christ (a name)	crist, Criste
Christ (Latin)	christum, christus
Christ's	cristes
cities	burgum
city	burch, byri
claw	clea
clean	clænan, clæne, clene
clear (Latin)	clara
clement (Latin)	clemens
cleverly-woven	geapneb
coal	col
cock's spur grass	attorlaþe
cold	cealde
come	cyme
comfort	fultum
comfrey	consolde
commanded	het
composed	gesette
conceal	forhelan
concealed	gehyded
conflict	niðweorca
conquered	geeode
consecrated	gehalgod
considers	geðenceð.

English	Ænglisc
Constantinus	constantinus
continuously	singalan
counsel	ræda
counted	rime, rimes
courageous	ellenrof
covered	belegde, bilegde, oferfæðmed
covering	hælon
created	gesceop, sceop, scop, wyrcean
creation	gesceap
creator	fruma, meotod, metod, ordfruma
creature	wiht
cross	Rod, rode
crowd	ðreat
Cuthbert	cudberch, cudberte

D, d

English	Ænglisc
dales	dalum
Danes	Dæne
dare	dyrre
dark	heolstre, wonne
darkness	sweartra, þystre
day	dæg, dæge
days	dagas
dear	deore, dyre
death	deað, deaþe
death-day	deaðdege, deoðdaege
deed	dæd, daed
deed-doer	dædfruma
deeds	dæda, dædum
deemed	demed, doemed, doemid
deeming	doma
deep	deope
deepen	diopian
deer	deora
defended	bewerode
delaying	agælde
delays	foręldit
delight	wyn
Derby	Deoraby
descendants	eafora

89

English	Ænglisc	English	Ænglisc
destroy	oðwyrceanne	*earth*	eorðan, eorðe, eorþan, eorþe, foldan, greot
destroyed	wyrde		
did	dydon., gedidon, gedydon	*easily*	eaþe
dies	swyltit	*east*	east
dill	dile	*Edgar*	eadgar
Dionisius	dionisius	*Edmund*	Eadmund
dispense	britnian	*Edmund's*	eadmundes
disposess	oðehtian	*Edward*	eadward, eadwarde, Eadweardes
distinguished	mære		
do	do, gedo	*elder*	ellen
do not	ne	*elders'*	aelda, eorðan
do-away	toscufeð	*elecampane*	eolone
does not	ne	*embraced*	ymbclyppað
doing	dydon	*end*	ende
domain	geweald	*enduring*	dreogeð
downwards	niþer	*Engla*	engla
drive	cnyssan, fere	*English*	Ænglisc, engla, feondscipe
drive-away	oðfeorrganne, oðfergean		
		enmity	feondscipe
drive-off	oðferie	*entrusted*	befæste
dung	scerne	*established*	astelidæ, onstealde
dwell	eardast, wunað	*eternal*	æce, æcum, ece, eci
dwelling	tun, wunian	*eternal (Latin)*	æterna, aeternus
dwelling place	eardwica	*evaporate*	weorne
dwellings	wycum	*even*	efne
dwelt	wunode	*ever*	a, simle
		everlasting	ece
		every	ealles, gehwam, gehwilce

E, e

		everything	æghwæt
e	e	*everything (Latin)*	omnia
each	ælcre, gehwæs, gehwilc, gihuaes	*evil*	yfeles, yfla, yflaes, yfles
Eadbert	eadberch	*exceedingly*	swiðe
Eadfrid	eadfrið	*excellence*	selast
Eadmund	Eadmund	*except*	butan, buton
Eadwacer (a name)	eadwacer	*excuse*	ladigan
eagerly	fultumes, georne	*expected*	wendest
eagle's	earnes	*eyes*	eagan
ear	eare		
earl	eorle		
earning	earnian, earnunga		
ears	eare		

F, f

		face	heafde
		fades-away (Latin)	abolescit
		fail	teorað

English	Ænglisc
fair	fæger
faith	geleafa, treowe
false	
famous	breome, mæra, mære
fares	fareð
far-wandering	widlastum
fasten	fæste
fastened	fæst
father	fæder
felterry	felterre
fen mint	fenminte
find	find, findan, findanne
finds	findeð
first	ær, ærest, aerist
fish	fisca
five	fife
flood	floda
fly	fleogan
folk	folc, folca
food	metes
food-lacking	meteliste
foot	fet, fot
foot-battle	feðewigges
for	for, fore, til, to
for a long time	longe
for a time	þrage
for days	dogode
for help	helpes
for the sake of	þurh
for you	þe
for-a-time	þrage
forever	symle
forgetfulness	æminde
for-men	firum
forth	forð, to
forwards	fundian
found	funde, inuenta
found (Latin)	inuenta
founded	gestaðolad
freedom	freodom
freely	freolic, freolice
frequently (Latin)	frequenter
friend	wine
from	a, ab, fram, of
from (Latin)	ab

English	Ænglisc
from below	nioþo
from me	æt
from there	þon, þonne
from-here	heonon
from-here-goes	heonengange, hiniongae, hinionge
from-there	þonne
full (Latin)	pleno

G, g

English	Ænglisc
Garmund (a name)	garmund
gathered	gegaderod
gave	gyfe
ghost	gæste
give	gief, syle, syllan
give worthiness to	geweorðad
gladly	geornor
glorious	tireadge
glory	blæd, dom, domę, wuldor, wuldres
glory-father	uuldurfadur, wuldorfæder
go to	to
god	gode
god (Latin)	deus
God-heathen's	godes
God's	godes, God's
going	agangen
gold	golde
good	fægere, god, godaes, godes
good (Latin)	bona
goods	duguðe
gracefully	geþungen
graciously	holdlice
grant	geunne
great	micel, micelan, miclum
great (Latin)	magna
greater	ma
great-king	þeodkyninges
grey	hare
gripped	gripe
grow	ace, aweox, waxsian
grown	gewæxen, gewexen

English	Ænglisc	English	Ænglisc
grows	ace	*heaven-kingdom's*	hefaenricaes, heofonrices
grows-cold	acolað	*heaven's*	swegles
grows-cold (Latin)	frigesscit	*heights*	alta
grows-dark	aðystrað	*heir-of*	afera
grows-dark (Latin)	obtenebrescit	*hell-fire-like*	hellfirena
grows-dirty	asolað	*help*	helpe, helpend
grows-dirty (Latin)	squalescit	*heralded*	bodade
grows-old	forealdað	*here*	her
grows-old (Latin)	senescunt	*Herod (a name)*	herod
guardian	mundbora	*hidden*	forhelan, forholen, gehided.

H, h

English	Ænglisc	English	Ænglisc
had	hæfde	*hidden (Latin)*	abscondita
Hagen's	hagenan	*high (Latin)*	ipselos
half	healfe	*highest (Latin)*	summi, summo, summus
hallowed	halgad	*high-ranking*	heahþungenum
hand	hand, handa	*hill*	berhge
hands	handa	*him*	him, hine
hand-worm's	handwurmes	*himself*	self, selfum, sylfum
hang	ho	*hipbone*	hupeban
hanged	ahangen	*his*	him, his, hys, sinum
happened	gelamp	*his child*	byre
harm	derian, sceððan	*his enemies*	feondum.
Harold	harolde	*his-self*	sylfan
has	hafað	*hit*	hælon
hasten	onette	*hoard-lock*	hordlocan
hating	feogan	*hold*	heald, healde
have	habbanne, habben, hafa, hauest	*holds (Latin)*	tenet
have mercy	gemiltsað	*holy*	haleg, halgan, halig, haligan, haligne
he	he, hie, him, hine, his, hit, hy, se	*holy (Latin)*	sanctæ
he was (Latin)	fuit	*holy one*	halgan
head	heafud	*holy water*	hæligwæter
healed	lacnað	*holy-book*	halgungboc
hear	gehyrest, hwæt	*home*	ham
heard	hyrde	*homeland*	eðle, eþeles
heart	heortan, mod	*honour*	hergan, herigean, wurðmynt
hearth	heorþe	*hopes*	wena, wenum
heat	hat	*horse*	hæncgest
heat (Latin)	ardor	*horse-collar*	haman
heathen	hæþenra	*hostile*	fah
heaven	heben, heofon, heofonum	*houses*	husa
		however	hwæþre
		Humber	Humbra

English	Ænglisc	English	Ænglisc
hundred	hun, hund	keep	weard
hung up	ahengon	keep-away	oðhealde
		keeper	hyrdes
		keeping	wæra
		kin	kynn
		kinds	kyn
		king	cyning, cyninge, cyninges, kinge, kyng

I, i

I	ic, mec
if	gif, gyf
in	in, inne, on, to
in pain	ermig
indeed	hwæt
inhabited	eardiæð
injury	andan
innumerable	ungerim
intend	þence
intent	ðence
intercede	þingian
interceded	geændade
into	in, innan
Iohannes	iohannes
is	est, is, sy
is (Latin)	est
is he	him
is led (Latin)	reducað, reducat
is named	hattæ
island	eglond, iege
islanders	igbuend
it	he, hi, him, hit, hyt, seo, þe, þis
it is	is

king (continued)

English	Ænglisc
king of	cyningc
king, king	cyning
kingdom	rice
kingdom (Latin)	regna
kings	cyninga
king's	cyninges
kinsman	mæg
kinsmen	mæcgea
know	cunne, wat

J, j

jewelled-sheath	stanfate
journey	liþan
joyfully	lustum
joys	dreamas, sibbe
Judas	ludeas
judge (Latin)	iudex
judgement	dom, domes
judgement-firm	domfæstne
just (Latin)	iustus

L, l

laid	legde
land	land, lande, landes
lands	foldan, foldu
lay	legge
lays	leg
lead-off	oðlædanne, oðlæde
leads	gelæde
leaf	leaf
learned	gleaw, lerde
learning	lara
led	reducant, reducat
left	wynstre
legacy	laf
Leicester	Ligoraceaster
let	ga
let it be so	fiað
let us	uton
life	feore, life
light	leoht, leohta, leohtes
light (Latin)	luce, lux
likened	gelicade
likewise	swylce
lily	lilie
limbs	liþu

K, k

English	*Ænglisc*	*English*	*Ænglisc*
Lincoln	Lincylene	*Mary*	marian
linseed	linsetcorn	*matters*	gehwilces
lion	leo	*Maximianus*	maximianus
little	litel, lytle	*may*	mæg, moten
little (Latin)	micro	*may be*	mæg
little wen	wenchichenne	*me*	me
live	wuniad	*meet with*	gemetað
living	lifgende	*meeting*	geanoðe
living (Latin)	uiuendo	*men*	manna, menn, niþþa, weras
loaned	læne		
loathsome	laþ	*Mercia*	myrce
long	lange	*merciful*	arfesta, milde
longer	leng	*middle-earth*	middangeard, middungeard
look	gebide		
lord	drihten, drihtne, dryctin, ealdor, frea, frean, hærran, hlaford, þeoden	*might*	maecti, meahte, mihta, mihtan, mihte, mihton, mihtum
		mighty	mihta
Lord's	drihnes	*mild*	milde
lost	losod	*mind*	hyge
love	leof, lofe, loue, lufianne, siblufan	*mindful*	gemindige, gemynde, gemyndi
love (Latin)	amor	*mind-plans*	modgeþanc, modgidanc
loyally	holdlice	*mind's*	modes
lupine	elehtre	*mine*	me, mines, minum
		ministers	minstre

M, m

		monk	muneca
made	gesceop, wyrican	*mood*	mod
made famous	gemærsod	*more*	ma
made-famous	gemærsod	*most*	mæst
maiden	mædenman, mægeð	*mournful*	geomres, murnende
maiden (Latin)	uirginis	*mournfully*	reotugu
maker (Latin)	factor	*much*	miccli, micel
Malchus	malchus	*murmuring*	niða
man	man, menn, wera	*my*	min, mines
mankind	moncynne, monnum		
mankind's	moncynnæs, moncynnes		

N, n

man's	mannes		
many	feola, manega, manegum, micel, monia, monig, monige	*nails*	næglas
		name	nama, nemnað, nemnaþ
marrabulum	marubie	*named*	hatte
marshmallow	merscmealwan	*names*	naman
Martimianus	martimianus	*nations*	ðeoda, þeoda
		necessary	þearf

English	*Ænglisc*	*English*	*Ænglisc*
neck	sweoran	of books	boca
needed-journey	nedfere, neidfaerae	of Christ	Christi
needs	ðearf, þarf, þearf	of heaven (Latin)	caelorum
neither	ne	of it	hit
never	næfre, nales	of land	lande
never (Latin)	nusquam	of man	wera
nevertheless	ac, þeah	of mind	mine
next	nihgan	of peace	gesælða
nigh	neah	of peace (Latin)	pacis
nights	nihtum	of the Anglo-Saxons	angolsexna
nine	nigon	of the Burgundians	burgenda
Nithad's	niðhades	of the poles (Latin)	polorum
nobility	æðele	of the world (Latin)	cosmi, mundi
noble	æðela, æðele, æðelum, æþelne, æþelre, æþelum	of virtues	kystum
		offer	lace
		offered	lac
nobleman	beorn	offertory	ofrað
nobler	æþelne	often	oft, oftor
noble's	æðelinges	of-that	þæs
none	næni, naenig, nænige, nenig	of-worth	weorðae, weorþe, wiorðe.
nor	ne	old	ealdan
north	norð, north	on	an, et, on
Northmen	Norðmannum	on me	me
not	nat, ne	once	Geo
not (Latin)	non	one	an, anum, man, mon
not at all	nalles	one (Latin)	unica
noted	gefrege	or	aeðða, oððe, oþþe
not-have	næbbe	ordered	het
nothing	nanuht, nawiht	origin	or
Nottingham	Snotingaham	ornaments	frætewum
now	Nu	Oswald's	osuualdes
number	gerimes	other	ec, oðres, oþer
numbered	gerimes, screoda, talade	our	uncer, urne
		ours	uncerne, userne
nurturing (Latin)	almum	out	ut
		out of	op
		outcast	wræclastum
		over	geond, ofer, on
		overcame	ofercom
		own	age

O, o

oaths	aðas		
obeyed	hyrde, hyrdon		
obtain	begytan		
ocean-stream	brimstream		
of	ðe, of, on		
of (Latin)	de		

P, p

		pass	eonene

English	Ænglisc	English	Ænglisc
passed	aurnen	recite	ongalan
peace	friþes	reckoned	geteled
pennyroyal	polleie	redeemer (Latin)	redemptor
Pentecost	pentecostenes	rejoice	gefeoh
people	leode	rejoicing	blis, dreame
perpetual	perhennem	released	alysde, forlet;
person's	mannes	relics	reliquia
Pharoah's	Farones	remain	lafe
pile	heap	remedy	læcedome
place of	stæl	rest	restað
poem	giedd	reward	iulean, lean
poet	sceop	riches	sinc
possessions	æhtum	right	swiðre, swiþran
power	mægenum	right now (Latin)	iamiamque
powerful (Latin)	dinamis	righteous	rædfæst, soþfæste
power-inside	encratea	rights	rhyta
powers	mihta	right-thinking	reþehygdig
praise	oliccan	river	ea
pray	bidde, bide	roomy	rume
pray (Latin)	rogo	rotten	syre
prevail	gefremede	royal-power	kyneþrymme
priests	preosta	rule over	wealdan
properly	ryhte	ruled	weoldon
property	ceap	ruler	waldend, wealdend
prosper	gedige	rules (Latin)	regit
prosperity	euthenia	ruling	weold
protect	witanne	ruling (Latin)	regentem
protecting	hleo		
protection-powers	mundcræftas		
protects	wereð		
pursued	fylgan		

Q, q

quenched	adwæsce
quietly	stille

R, r

rainy	renig
raise	aræred
raise up	arær
ready	gearo, recon
receive	fo, onfo

S, s

said	gecwæð
saint	sancte
saintly	sanctus
sake-of	þurh
salvation (Latin)	salus
sat	sæt
satisfaction	frofre
saviour	hæleða, nergend
say	cweð, cweðe, cweþ, cweþe, Cwyð, secgað, seggeð
saying	cwæð, cwet
says	secge
seized	genam
seldom-coming	seldcymas

English	Ænglisc	English	Ænglisc
sense (Latin)	sensu	*sound*	rædfest
sent	onsended, sende	*south*	suð
separate	getwæmde	*speak*	cweðan
Serafion	serafion	*spirit*	ferðe, gast, gastae, gastæ, gaste, modsefan
seven	seofon, vii		
shall	sceal, scealt		
shall be	beoð	*splendid*	freolice
shall-we	sculon, scylun	*spoke*	gyddode, maðelode
shaper	scepen, scyppend	*spoken*	gesæd
she	heo	*sprout*	crop
shield	helme	*Stamford*	Stanford
shines	scine	*stands*	standeð
shining	scan	*steps*	steppa
shining (Latin)	nitor	*stolen*	forstolen, stolenne
should	sceal, scolde	*stones*	stanas
shoulders	eaxelum	*stood*	stode
shrink	clinge	*storms*	scurum
shrivel	scring	*strawberry*	streawbergean
sick-person	adlegan	*strength (Latin)*	fortis
sin	firene, synna	*strengths*	mægen
since	syððan	*strong*	stronge
sing	sing, singan	*strong souled*	modhwatu
singed	inswiden	*subjected*	nyde
sink	sigað	*successful*	sigisiþa
sister	sweostar	*such*	hwylce, swylce
sit	sitte	*such as*	swylce
sitting on (Latin)	sedentem	*suddenly*	lungre
six	siex	*supplicant (Latin)*	supplex
skilful	cræftig	*support*	fylste, gioce
slack	lata	*surely*	huru
smaller	lesse	*surged*	scyndeð
so	se, swa, þæs	*surrounded*	biþeaht, biworpen
so long as	þenden	*swarming*	swirman
soak	ofgeot	*swept-away*	fornam
someone	mon	*Sword*	mece, mecum
sometimes	hwilum	*swore*	swor
somewhere	earne		
son	bearn, bearnum, sunu		
son (Latin)	filius		
soon	sona		
sorrel	docce		
soul	hyge, saule, sawle		
soul-hoard	feorhhord		
souls	sawla		
souls (Latin)	animæ		

T, t

English	Ænglisc
take	feta, fo, fone, nim, niman
taken	genam
tears-apart	tosliteð
teary	tearige
tell	saga, secgan

English	Ænglisc	English	Ænglisc
temptation	costunga	the prince	þeodne
ten	tyn	the proud	wlance
than	ðon, þan, þonne	the ruling king	þrymcyningc
thane	ðegen	the saints (Latin)	sancti
thank	geþancie, þance	the Saxons	sexum
that	ða, ðær, ðæt, ðam, ðe, þa, þæm, þæs, þæt, þætte, þam, þam, þe, þet, þon	the Scots	scottum
		the south	meridie
		the south (Latin)	austro
that are	is	the throne	thronum
the	ða, ðæm, ðaem, ðam, ðe, ðene, ði, hi, him, se, seo, þa, þaem, þæne, þæs, þæt, þam, þam, þan, þe, þone	the virgin (Latin)	uirginem
		the Wear	weor
		the Welsh	walum
		the west	occidente
		the west (Latin)	occidente
		the wolf's	wolues
the Angles	englum	the woods	wuda
the best	betest	the world	cosmo, worulda
the book (Latin)	biblos	the world (Latin)	mundum, orbem
the Britons	bryttum	the world's (Latin)	mundi
the country	edygled	the wound	benne
the cross	crucem, Crux	the young	geong
the cross (Latin)	crux	the-birth	gebyrdtide
the Danes	dena	the-chamber	in
the day	dæg	the-Creator, the-Creator	metode
the dear	deore		
The Dore	Dor	their	hyra
the dwarf's	dweores	the-lord	dryhten, dryhtne, þeoden
the eagle's	earnes		
the earth	eorðan, eorþan	them	þam
the east	oriente	the-measurer's	meotodes, metudæs
the east (Latin)	oriente	then	ða, ðonne, þa, tha, þænne, þe, þon, þone, þonne
the end	finit		
the hallows	halewæge		
the heavens	rodores	thenceforth	siþþan
the host	rimde	Theodric	ðeodric
the innocent	bealuleas	there	ðær, ðære, ðer, þær, þer, þonne
the island	ige		
the king	kingc	therefore	þi
the king (Latin)	regem	these	ðem, hire, þas
the Lord	drihten, dryhtne	the-world	worulde
the middle	midd	they	ðem, hi, hy, sunt, þæm
the name	noma		
the north (Latin)	aquilone	they are	sindon
the pain	dolh	they-are (Latin)	sunt
the people	folces, leodum	thing	þinga
		think	gehicgenne, þence, wene

English	Ænglisc	English	Ænglisc
thirty	xxx	too	eac
this	ðeos, ðere, ðes, ðis, þæs, þas, þeos, þis, þyos	took	genom
		top-of-the-head	moldan
		to-thee	ðe
this wound	benne	town	burh, buruh, byrig
thistle	þystel	trappings	geatwum
those	þone, þonne	treasure	maðma
though	þe, þeah	treasures	madma
thought	ðohte, geþohte, þances	trees	treowum
		trembling	byfigynde
thoughts	gemind	troops	weorudes
thought-wiser	ðonosnottorra, þoncsnotturra	true	
		truly	soð
thousand	ðusend	trusted-friends	treowgeþofta
three	þry, þrym	trusts	gelifeð
three times	þriwa	truth-fastened	soðfæsta, soðfæstan
three-times	III, þriwa	truth-firm	soðfæst
thrive	geþeoh	turn	gecyrre, hweorfað
throb	hoppettan	twenty	twentig, xx
thrones	throno	twenty four	xxiiii
through	ðurh, þurh	twenty-eight	xxviii
throw	forweorp		
throw down	oferweorp		
Thureth	þureð		

U, u

English	Ænglisc
thus	ðus, swa, þus
ties	teage
time	tid, tiid
titled	teode, tiadæ
to	to
to be	wæs
to kill	aþecgan
to look	locian
to me	me
to send	onsendon
to the	þære
to us	us
to Widia	widian
to Wulf (a name)	wulfes
to you	þine
to-be	siae, sie, sy
together	geador, gemonge, gesomnad
to-him	him
told	secgan
to-mark	gemearcian
tongue	tungan

English	Ænglisc
under	under
undertake	ongunn
undertaking	gahwem
universal	gemæne
unknowing	uncuþ
unlike	ungelic, ungelice
unnumbered	unarimeda
unrelated	unmægas
until	oðþæt, oþ
upon us	us
us	us, usic, ussum

V, v

English	Ænglisc
vessel	hordfate
vestment	reaf
victories	sigora
victorious-women	sigewif
victory	sige
virtue	duguðe

English	Ænglisc	English	Ænglisc
virtue (Latin)	uirtute	*who (Latin)*	quem, qui
voice (Latin)	uoce	*wide*	rumre, widan, wide
		widely	wide
		Widia	widia
W, w		*wild*	wilda, wilde
		will	willa, willað
wafer	oflætan	*will (Latin)*	uoluntate
wafers	oflætan	*will-be*	wiorðeð, wiurðit, wyrþeþ
Waldere	waldere		
walking	gangan	*willing*	wile
ward	uard, weard	*wing*	ueþer
warrior	wiga	*winters*	wintra
warriors	oretmægcum, wiggendra	*winters-numbered*	wintergeteles
		wise	froda
was	wæs, wes	*wiser*	snotera
was hidden	abscondita	*wishes*	wyle
waste-away	weornie, weornige	*with*	mid, midd
water	wætre, weter	*with (Latin)*	cum
water elf disease	wæterælfadle	*with them*	heom
wave	yþ	*wither away*	geweornie
waves	brymmas, yðum	*withers*	onbere
waxed	weox	*within*	binnan, innan
we	we	*without*	butan
wealth	welan, weolan	*wonder*	uundra, wundra
weapon	hildefrofre	*wondrous*	wuldres, wundorlicne, wundrum
weather	weder		
weight (Latin)	pondus	*wondrously*	wundrum
Weland's	welandes	*wood*	wudu
well	wel	*wood-fastened*	wudafæstern
wellbeing	godes	*word*	word, worde
welling	weallendan	*words*	wordum
well-known	gecyðed	*word-vows*	wordbeot
wen	wenne	*work*	labor, weorcum
were	wæran, wære	*work (Latin)*	ponus
west	west	*work-of*	uerc, weorc
wet	bestemed	*works*	gehwylcre
what	hwæt	*world*	gesceaft, woruld
what-of	huaet, hwæt, hwet	*world-kingdom*	woruldrice
when	ðonne, þa, þonne	*wormwood*	wermod
whenever	þonne	*worst*	wyrrestan, wyrstan
whereby	þonne	*worth*	wurðe
which	ðe, hwilcne, þe	*worth-minded*	weorðmynda
which (Latin)	que	*worthship*	weorþscipe
white	hwit	*wound*	wund
Whitwell Gap	Hwitanwyllesgeat	*wounds*	wunde
who	ðe, hwa, se	*wrathfully*	wraþe

English	Ænglisc
write	writan
writer of books	bocera
writings	gewritu, writ
wrote	awrat
Wulf (a name)	wulf

Y, y

yet	ðeah, gen
yew berry	eowberge
you	ðu, eow, ge, þe, þu
young and brave	hagestealde
your	þin, þine, þinne, þinre, þinum
yours	þinre, þinum
youth	gecheðe
youth's	geonges

Books by the Author

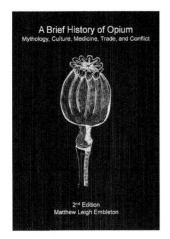

A Brief History of Opium: Mythology, Culture, Medicine, Trade, and Conflict

Ideas about the origin of humankind's relationship with the opium poppy are complex and varied, and the further back in time we look, the more hypotheses and speculation we find filling in the gaps. Perhaps this strangest and most mysterious of plants has the power to vividly inspire the imagination as much in the study of its history, as with the generation of Romantic Poets who believed that its extracts stimulated their imagination to write a new genre of poetry filled with visual imagery.

From ancient civilisations of the Neolithic period to the present day, the opium poppy (*Papaver Somniferum*) has a fascinating history, from iconic associations with the dark symbolism of trance, sleep, dreams, and death in Greco-Roman mythology, to the search for ever stronger pain relief without the dangers of addiction in modern medicine.

Since its discovery and description as a powerful painkiller in ancient medical texts, to the battlefields of the American Civil War, 'God's Own Medicine' has been both a blessing and a curse for humankind. The growth and profitability of the opium trade has caused wars, and funded others. It has relieved pain for some, but been the cause of pain and suffering for others. Its illicit recreational use, subsequent addiction, and complex issues of war and politics have plagued humankind to this day.

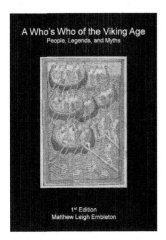

A Who's Who of the Viking Age: People, Legends, and Myths

Who were the players? Where do they exist on the scale of history, legend, and myth? And how do we know? From the first raids by the mysterious 'Northmen' in the darkness of the 8th century, to the chieftains, earls, and kings who changed the development of Europe and influenced the medieval world, the Viking Age produced stories and accounts of unique figures in history preserved in oral tradition, and written in chronicles, and sagas.

With a distinctive culture, shaped by the bleak and unforgiving landscape of Nothern Europe, the character and outlook of the Norse people was driven by the brutal reality of a struggle for land, resources, and survival. The varied geography of Scandinavia with its fjords, mountains, lakes, islands, and marshlands set the stage for developments in seafaring and boat building that were far ahead of the rest of Europe, allowing the bold and adventurous to travel further and further afield in search of routes for exploration, plunder, trade, and settlement.

Those who raided are today known as Vikings, a term coined in the 18th century at the beginning of a period of renewed interest in local mythology and folklore as a means of national identity (the Old Norse word '*víkingr*' meant a sea-rover or a pirate). The sagas and stories of their activities were translated and later embellished to fit romantic ideals of the heroic warrior or the noble savage. Many of the popular misconceptions about the Vikings and the Viking Age come from this period.

The aim of this book is to outline who they were, what we know about them, and how each of these figures shaped the story of the age, with quotations from contemporary and near-contemporary sources.

Anglo-Saxon Poems, Charms, and Proverbs: Old English Text, Translation, and Word List

Old English (*Ænglisc*) is the earliest recorded form of the English language. As a West Germanic language, it was brought to Great Britain by Anglo-Saxon settlers in the mid-5th century, and the first literary works date from the mid 7th century.

'Chronicle Poems' found in the Anglo-Saxon Chronicles comment on significant events such as *The Capture of the Five Boroughs*, *The Coronation of Edgar*, and *The Death of Edward (the Confessor)*.

'Metrical Charms' contained recipes and instructions designed to magically resolve a situation or illness, with some sort of action, a medical potion, and chanting and repeating special phrases, such as Charm No.03 *Against a Dwarf* (*fever*), No.05 *For Loss of Cattle*, No.07 *For the Water-Elf Disease*, No.08 *For a Swarm of Bees*, No.09 *For Loss of Cattle*, No.10 *For Loss of Cattle*, and No.12 *Against a Wen*.

'The Exeter Book' is a major manuscript of poetry believed to have been produced in the late 10th century, and includes the poems *Pharaoh*, *Alms-Giving*, *The Lord's Prayer I*, *The Partridge*, *Homiletic Fragment II*, and *Wulf and Eadwacer*.

Other Poems include: *A Proverb from Winfrid's Time*, *The Gloria II*, *Bede's Death Song* (*Northumbrian Version*), *Bede's Death Song* (*The Hague Version*), *Bede's Death Song* (*West Saxon Version*), *Latin-English Proverbs*, *The Brussels Cross*, *Caedmon's Hymn* (*Northumbrian Version*), *Caedmon's Hymn* (*West Saxon Version*), *Thureth*, *Aldhelm*, *Durham*, *A Summons to Prayer*, and *Waldere B*.

This book is designed to be of use to anyone studying or with a keen interest in Anglo-Saxon or Old English, clearly showing how the languages works, and the beginnings of what would evolve into modern English. This edition is laid out in three columns, the original text, a literal word-for-word translation, a modern translation, and individual word lists for each poem. Also included is an overall word list with over 1,000 definitions.

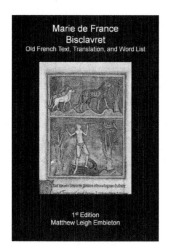

Marie de France – Bisclavret: Old French Text, Translation, and Word List

This 12th century poem tells the story of a nobleman with a dark secret; he disappears for days at a time, for he is a werewolf. Bisclavret is a poetic tale of love, betrayal, the supernatural, and courtly romance.

Marie de France (fl 1160 to 1215) was a poet born in France who lived in England during the late 12th century. She was well known at the Plantagenet royal court of King Henry II of England and Eleanor of Aquitaine, and she is believed to have been an abbess of a monastery.

Her poems or 'Lais' are believed to have been written sometime between 1160 and 1175 drawing upon Breton and Arthurian myths and legends. They are written in a form of Old French known as 'Anglo-Norman', which came from 'Old Norman', part of the 'Langues d'oïl' dialect continuum of Gallo-Romance languages.

Old French is the result of a gradual separation from Vulgar Latin and Common Romance, coming into contact with influences from Gaulish (Continental Celtic), and Frankish (Germanic). The Lais were later translated into Old Norse for a collection known as 'Strengleikar' commissioned by King Haakon IV of Norway.

This edition is laid out in three columns, the original text, a literal word-for-word translation, and a modern translation. Also included is a word list with over 1,000 definitions.

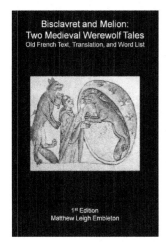

Bisclavret and Melion: Two Medieval Werewolf Tales: Old French Text, Translation, and Word List

Bisclavret was written by Marie de France between 1160 and 1175, while Melion was written by an unknown or anonymous writer between 1190 and 1204. While they are several decades apart, they have a number of similarities. This has led some people to believe that they could in fact originate from the same story, or perhaps they are both inventions drawing on the same source of icons and motifs found in the folklore, myth, and legends of the time.

These 'lais' were popular in the courts of Europe in the late medieval period, drawing particularly on Breton and Arthurian myths and legends, which often contained elements of the supernatural to ornament what were moral tales of heroism and chivalry.

They are both written in Old French, Bisclavret is in 'Anglo-Norman', whereas Melion is in the 'Picard dialect', both of which are part of the 'Langues d'oïl' dialect continuum of Gallo-Romance languages.

Old French is the result of a gradual separation from Vulgar Latin and Common Romance, coming into contact with influences from Gaulish (Continental Celtic), and Frankish (Germanic).

This edition is laid out in three columns, the original text, a literal word-for-word translation, and a modern translation. Also included is a word list with over 1,000 definitions.

Galdrastafir (*English Edition*): A Collection of Icelandic Magical Staves

The Galdrastafir that survive in various manuscripts from the Late Middle Ages until the 20th Century give us a glimpse of a rich tradition of magic in the Norse world. From the formulation of runes into bindrunes and ever more complex magical symbols, to the incorporation of references to biblical seals and elements of the Christian faith, the relationship between traditional magic and religious symbolism is a complex and varied one.

From the positive invocations of good luck, success, wealth, etc. to the protection of one's person or property from theft or magic, to darker and more morally complex intentions, these symbols are shown here to provide a broad view of the people's concerns and how the practitioners of magic attempted to address these concerns in Iceland in the Late Medieval and Early Modern periods. The things our ancestors wished for, the concerns they sought solution to, the magic they believed in to make it happen, and the way the symbols and spells were formulated and practiced, tell us about who we are, and where we have come from.

Galdrastafir (*Swedish Edition*): En Samling av Isländska Magiska Rungalder

Galdrastafir som överlever i olika manuskript från sen medeltid fram till 1900-talet ger oss en glimt av en rik tradition av magi i den norra världen. Från formuleringen av runor till bindrunorna och allt mer komplexa magiska symboler, till införlivandet av referenser till bibliska sälar och delar av den kristna tron, förhållandet mellan traditionell magi och religiös symbolik är en komplex och varierad.

Från de positiva åkallelserna av lycka till, framgång, rikedom osv, för att skydda ens person eller egendom från stöld eller magi, till mörkare och mer moraliskt komplexa avsikter, dessa symboler visas här för att ge en bred vy av folkets oro och hur utövare av magi försökte ta itu med dessa problem på Island under sent i medeltiden och tidigt modern tid.

Det som våra förfäder önskade, de bekymmer de sökte lösningen på, magin de trodde på för att få det att hända, och hur symbolerna och trollformlerna formulerades och övades, berätta om vem vi är och var vi har kommit ifrån.

Havamal, Sayings of The High One: Norse Text, Translation, and Word List

The Hávamál ('sayings of the high one' i.e. 'Odin') is a collection of poetry from the Viking age. It can be described as 'gnomic poetry' in that it contains a series of insightful verses which offer advice in the form of maxims and aphorisms (short statements, observations, and opinions) about how to live one's life, how to conduct oneself in a proper manner, and how to gain and use wisdom in order to survive and prosper in a dangerous world.

It is an important source of Old Norse philosophy, an insight into the minds of the people of the Norse world, and an important source of mythology concerning the origin of the runes, and their importance and significance in Norse culture which continues to this day.

It is preserved in the 'Codex Regius' ('Royal Book', 'King's Book', 'Konungsbók' (GKS 2365 4to) which has been dated to around c1260-1280, but the poetry itself has been variously dated back as far as the 10th or even 9th century.

This book is designed to be of use to anyone studying or with a keen interest in Old Norse or Old Icelandic, clearly showing how these languages work, and the influence of these languages on English.

This edition is laid out in three columns, the original text, a literal word-for-word translation, and a modern translation. Also included is a word list with over 1,000 definitions.

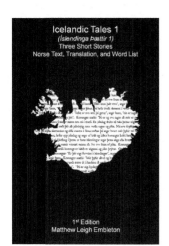

Icelandic Tales 1 (*Íslendinga þættir 1*): Three Short Stories, Norse Text, Translation, and Word List

The meaning of the word 'saga' (plural: 'sǫgur' or 'sögur') translates as 'that which is said', or more widely: a 'saying', 'statement', 'story', 'tale', or 'narrative'. Also in the storytelling tradition of medieval Iceland is the short story called the 'þáttr' (plural: 'þættir'), meaning a strand of rope or a yarn, comparable to the word 'yarn' in English sometimes used to refer to a story.

The three tales in this book are:

- The Tale of The Story-Wise Icelander (Íslendings Þáttr Sögufróða), a tale about a young Icelandic storyteller in the court of Harald Sigurdsson.

- The Tale of Thorstein Shiver (Þorsteins Þáttr Skelks), a tale about Thorstein Thorkelsson encountering a demon while feasting with King Olaf Tryggvason.

- The Tale of Ale-Hood (Ölkofra Þáttr), a satire on the legal and judicial system of the Icelandic Commonwealth, and its domination and manipulation by powerful individuals for their own financial gain, trampling over the rights of the people they are meant to protect.

This book is designed to be of use to anyone studying or with a keen interest in Old Norse or Old Icelandic, clearly showing how these languages work, and the influence of these languages on English.

This edition is laid out in three columns, the original text, a literal word-for-word translation, and a modern translation. Also included is a word list with over 1,000 definitions.

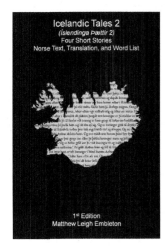

Icelandic Tales 2 (*Íslendinga þættir 2*): Four Short Stories, Norse Text, Translation, and Word List

The meaning of the word '*saga*' (plural: '*sǫgur*' or '*sögur*') translates as 'that which is *said*', or more widely: a 'saying', 'statement', 'story', 'tale', or 'narrative'. Also in the storytelling tradition of medieval Iceland is the short story called the '*þáttr*' (plural: '*þættir*'), meaning a strand of rope or a yarn, comparable to the word 'yarn' in English sometimes used to refer to a story.

The four tales in this book are:
- The Tale of Ívarr Son of Ingimundr (Ívars Þáttr Ingimundarsonar), a tale about a king who goes to great lengths to comfort his heartbroken friend.
- The Tale of Thidrandi and Thorhall (Þiðranda Þáttr ok Þórhalls), a tale about a sacrifice taken by spirits of the old gods, as their days are numbered due to the onset of christianity in Iceland.
- The Tale of Helga Thorisson (Helga Þáttr Þórissonar), a tale of two brothers who travel north on a trading voyage, coming into contact with powerful sorcery.
- The Tale of Audun of the West Fjords (Auðunar Þáttr Vestfirska), a tale of a poor man who makes a name for himself with an unusual gift and an epic journey.

This book is designed to be of use to anyone studying or with a keen interest in Old Norse or Old Icelandic, clearly showing how these languages work, and the influence of these languages on English.

This edition is laid out in three columns, the original text, a literal word-for-word translation, and a modern translation. Also included is a word list with over 1,000 definitions.

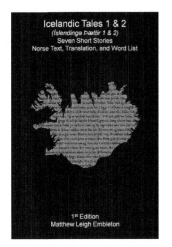

Icelandic Tales 1 & 2 (*Íslendinga þættir 1 & 2*): Seven Short Stories, Norse Text, Translation, and Word List

The meaning of the word '*saga*' (plural: '*sǫgur*' or '*sögur*') translates as 'that which is *said*', or more widely: a 'saying', 'statement', 'story', 'tale', or 'narrative'. Also in the storytelling tradition of medieval Iceland is the short story called the '*þáttr*' (plural: '*þættir*'), meaning a strand of rope or a yarn, comparable to the word 'yarn' in English sometimes used to refer to a story.

The seven tales in this double edition are:
- The Tale of The Story-Wise Icelander (Íslendings Þáttr Sögufróða), a tale about a young Icelandic storyteller in the court of Harald Sigurdsson.
- The Tale of Thorstein Shiver (Þorsteins Þáttr Skelks), a tale about Thorstein Thorkelsson encountering a demon while feasting with King Olaf Tryggvason.
- The Tale of Ale-Hood (Ölkofra Þáttr), a satire on the legal and judicial system of the Icelandic Commonwealth, by pointing to its domination and manipulation by powerful individuals for their own financial gain, trampling over the rights of the people they are meant to protect.
- The Tale of Ívarr Son of Ingimundr (Ívars Þáttr Ingimundarsonar), a tale about a king who goes to great lengths to comfort his heartbroken friend.
- The Tale of Thidrandi and Thorhall (Þiðranda Þáttr ok Þórhalls), a tale about a sacrifice taken by spirits of the old gods, as their days are numbered due to the onset of christianity in Iceland.
- The Tale of Helga Thorisson (Helga Þáttr Þórissonar), a tale of two brothers who travel north on a trading voyage, coming into contact with powerful sorcery.
- The Tale of Audun of the West Fjords (Auðunar Þáttr Vestfirska), a tale of a poor man who makes a name for himself with an unusual gift and an epic journey.

This book is designed to be of use to anyone studying or with a keen interest in Old Norse or Old Icelandic, clearly showing how these languages work, and the influence of these languages on English. This edition is laid out in three columns, the original text, a literal word-for-word translation, and a modern translation. Also included is a word list with over 1,000 definitions.

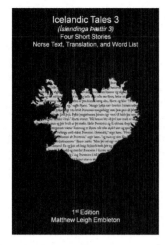

Icelandic Tales 3 (*Íslendinga þættir 3*): Four Short Stories, Norse Text, Translation, and Word List

The meaning of the word '*saga*' (plural: '*sǫgur*' or '*sögur*') translates as 'that which is *said*', or more widely: a 'saying', 'statement', 'story', 'tale', or 'narrative'. Also in the storytelling tradition of medieval Iceland is the short story called the '*þáttr*' (plural: '*þættir*'), meaning a strand of rope or a yarn, comparable to the word 'yarn' in English sometimes used to refer to a story.

The four tales in this book are:

- The Tale of Thorstein the Staff-Struck (Þorsteins þáttr stangarhǫggs), a tale of conflict, intergenerational honour, feud, and reconciliation.
- The Tale of Halldor Snorrason II (Halldórs þáttr Snorrasonar inn síðari), a tale of courtly pride and age old friendship.
- The Tale of Thorleif, the Earl's Poet (Þorleifs þáttr jarlsskálds), a cautionary tale of poetry and witchcraft.
- The Tale of Hreidar the Fool (Hreiðars þáttr heimska), a tale about a gentle giant who discovers himself and earns himself a reputation and land in the process.

This book is designed to be of use to anyone studying or with a keen interest in Old Norse or Old Icelandic, clearly showing how these languages work, and the influence of these languages on English.

This edition is laid out in three columns, the original text, a literal word-for-word translation, and a modern translation. Also included is a word list with over 1,000 definitions.

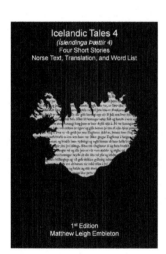

Icelandic Tales 4 (*Íslendinga þættir 4*): Four Short Stories, Norse Text, Translation, and Word List

The meaning of the word '*saga*' (plural: '*sǫgur*' or '*sögur*') translates as 'that which is *said*', or more widely: a 'saying', 'statement', 'story', 'tale', or 'narrative'. Also in the storytelling tradition of medieval Iceland is the short story called the '*þáttr*' (plural: '*þættir*'), meaning a strand of rope or a yarn, comparable to the word 'yarn' in English sometimes used to refer to a story.

The four tales in this book are:

- The Tale of Star-Oddi's Dream (Stjörnu-Odda draumr)
- The Tale of Bolli Bollason (Bolla þáttr Bollasonar)
- The Tale of Thorstein House-Power (Þorsteins þáttr bæjarmagns)
- The Tale of Sarcastic Halli (Sneglu-Halla þáttr)

This book is designed to be of use to anyone studying or with a keen interest in Old Norse or Old Icelandic, clearly showing how these languages work, and the influence of these languages on English.

This edition is laid out in three columns, the original text, a literal word-for-word translation, and a modern translation. Also included is a word list with over 1,000 definitions.

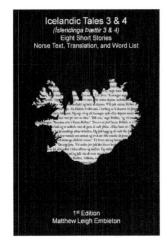

Icelandic Tales 3 & 4 (*Íslendinga þættir 3 & 4*): Four Short Stories, Norse Text, Translation, and Word List

The meaning of the word '*saga*' (plural: '*sǫgur*' or '*sögur*') translates as 'that which is *said*', or more widely: a 'saying', 'statement', 'story', 'tale', or 'narrative'. Also in the storytelling tradition of medieval Iceland is the short story called the '*þáttr*' (plural: '*þættir*'), meaning a strand of rope or a yarn, comparable to the word 'yarn' in English sometimes used to refer to a story.

The eight tales in this double edition are:

- The Tale of Thorstein the Staff-Struck (Þorsteins þáttr stangarhǫggs), a tale of conflict, intergenerational honour, feud, and reconciliation.
- The Tale of Halldor Snorrason II (Halldórs þáttr Snorrasonar inn síðari), a tale of courtly pride and age old friendship.
- The Tale of Thorleif, the Earl's Poet (Þorleifs þáttr jarlsskálds), a cautionary tale of poetry and witchcraft.
- The Tale of Hreidar the Fool (Hreiðars þáttr heimska), a tale about a gentle giant who discovers himself and earns himself a reputation and land in the process.
- The Tale of Star-Oddi's Dream (Stjörnu-Odda draumr)
- The Tale of Bolli Bollason (Bolla þáttr Bollasonar)
- The Tale of Thorstein House-Power (Þorsteins þáttr bæjarmagns)
- The Tale of Sarcastic Halli (Sneglu-Halla þáttr)

This book is designed to be of use to anyone studying or with a keen interest in Old Norse or Old Icelandic, clearly showing how these languages work, and the influence of these languages on English.

This edition is laid out in three columns, the original text, a literal word-for-word translation, and a modern translation. Also included is a word list with over 1,000 definitions.

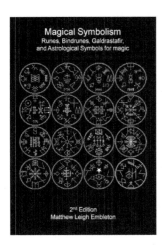

Magical Symbolism (*English Edition*): Runes, Bindrunes, Galdrastafir, and Astrological Symbols for Magic

Magical symbols are a fascinating example of the ingenuity of language, communication, and symbolic meaning. They show us human nature's attempt to use them as tools of expression, a divinatory means to understand the forces that exist all around us that shape our lives, and our attempts to influence these forces by signifying our intentions to the divine and the universe. They are an expression of the human spirit. They are part of us.

Magic works because we believe that it works. We believe in the process of signalling and communicating our intentions and desirable outcomes to the forces around us, releasing them into the universe, and having the confidence and belief to make it happen.

The aim of this book is to explore the traditions of magical symbols both from the Norse world, and the Greco-Roman world of antiquity, and its later revival in the Medieval and Renaissance periods.

From the linguistic origins of runes found in the Ancient Italic alphabets in the 1st century B.C.E, to the manuscripts preserved in the Byzantine Empire in the Middle Ages, to the revival and flourishing of both traditions in manuscripts, books, and notebooks during and after the Renaissance, two different cultures from the north and south of the continent give us a glimpse of our collective psyche, the characteristics of the deities that each culture recognised as reflections of our nature, and our belief in the power of symbols and magic.

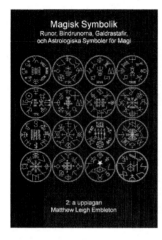

Magisk Symbolik (*Swedish Edition*): Runor, Bindrunorna, Galdrastafir, och Astrologiska Symboler för Magi

Magiska symboler är ett fascinerande exempel på uppfinningsrikedom i språk, kommunikation och symbolisk betydelse. De visar oss den mänskliga naturens försök att använda dem som uttrycksverktyg, ett divinerande sätt att förstå de krafter som finns runt omkring oss som formar våra liv, och våra försök att påverka dessa krafter genom att beteckna våra avsikter för det gudomliga och universum. De är ett uttryck för den mänskliga anden. De är en del av oss.

Magi fungerar för att vi tror att det fungerar. Vi tror på processen att signalera och kommunicera våra avsikter och önskvärda resultat till krafterna omkring oss, släppa dem i universum och ha förtroende och tro på att få det att hända.

Syftet med denna bok är att utforska traditionerna för magiska symboler både från den nordiska världen och den grekisk-romerska antikens värld och dess senare återupplivning under Medeltiden och Renässansen.

Från det språkliga ursprunget till runor som hittades i de forntida Italisk alfabeten under 1000-talet f.Kr., till manuskript som bevarats i det Bysantinska Riket under Medeltiden, till återupplivande och blomning av båda traditionerna i manuskript, böcker och anteckningsböcker under och efter Renässansen, två olika kulturer från norra och södra delen av kontinenten, ger oss en glimt av vår kollektiva psyk, egenskaperna hos de gudar som varje kultur erkände som reflektioner av vår natur och vår tro på kraften i symboler och magi.

Melion: A Medieval Werewolf Tale: Old French Text, Translation, and Word List

The author of Melion is unknown, but it is believed to have been written some time between 1190 and 1204.

It is one of around 10 anonymous 'lais' of that time drawing upon Breton and Arthurian myths and legends.

These myths and legends often contained elements of the supernatural to ornament what were moral tales of heroism and chivalry.

It is written in the Picard dialect of Old French, part of the 'Langues d'oïl' dialect continuum of Gallo-Romance languages.

Old French is the result of a gradual separation from Vulgar Latin and Common Romance, coming into contact with influences from Gaulish (Continental Celtic), and Frankish (Germanic).

This edition is laid out in three columns, the original text, a literal word-for-word translation, and a modern translation. Also included is a word list with over 1,000 definitions.

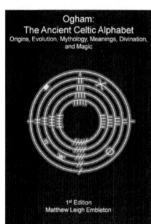

Ogham: The Ancient Celtic Alphabet: Origins, Evolution, Mythology, Meanings, Divination, and Magic

Ogham is an ancient Celtic writing system, alphabet, or cipher that was primarily designed to inscript Archaic Irish (sometimes called Primitive Irish), later Old Irish, and some Pictish and Old Welsh.

As well as having origins documented in the fields of history, linguistics, and archaeology, it also has a history of magic and mythology in Ancient Celtic Religion or Celtic Paganism.

Since the 20th century, there has been a revival of interest in this and other ancient polytheistic religions and spiritual practices by a growing number of Pagan or Neo-Pagan communities across the world.

It is the aim of this book to provide the bigger picture about where these symbols have come from, how they have developed, how they have been used, and how their use has evolved over two thousand years.

While there has been some division between the world of scholars and adacemics on one hand, and pagans, neo-pagans, etc, on the other, the author has attempted to present both sides as fully as possible while remaining neutral, leaving space for the reader to make up their own mind on the matter.

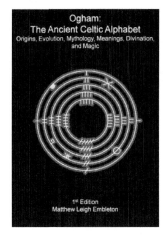

Ogham: Det Antika Keltiska Alfabetet: *(SwedishEdition):* Ursprung, Utveckling, mytologi, betydelser, spådom och magi

Ogham är ett forntida keltiskt skriftsystem, alfabet eller chiffer som i första hand utformades för att inskriva Arkaisk Irländska (ibland kallad Primitiv Irländska), senare Gammal Irländska och en del Piktisk och Gammal Walesisk.

Förutom att ha sitt ursprung dokumenterat inom områdena historia, lingvistik och arkeologi, har den också en historia av magi och mytologi inom antik Keltisk religion eller Keltisk hedendom.

Sedan 1900-talet har intresset för denna och andra forntida polyteistiska religioner och andliga sedvänjor återuppstått av ett växande antal hedniska eller nyhedniska samhällen över hela världen.

Det är syftet med den här boken att ge en större bild av var dessa symboler har kommit ifrån, hur de har utvecklats, hur de har använts och hur deras användning har utvecklats under två tusen år.

Även om det har funnits en viss uppdelning mellan världen av forskare och akademiker å ena sidan, och hedningar, neo-hedningar, etc, å andra sidan, har författaren försökt att presentera båda sidor så fullständigt som möjligt samtidigt som han förblir neutral, vilket lämnar utrymme för läsaren att bestämma sig.

Old Norse Word List: A Brief Glossary of 10,000 Old Norse and Old Icelandic Words

Old Norse is a North Germanic language spoken by inhabitants of Scandinavia from about the 7th to the 15th centuries. It has today evolved into the modern languages of Icelandic, Faroese, Norwegian, Danish, and Swedish.

During the Viking Age it also had an impact and influence on the English language which resulted in the simplification of its grammar, and many loan words which are still in use today.

The aim of this book is to be useful to anyone wishing to study, read, and understand the fascinating wealth of Old Norse and Old Icelandic literature available in its original form.

In this book there are over 10,000 words included (in both Norse to English and English to Norse format), as well as notes on the main word form differences between Old Norse and Old Icelandic, and the use of numbers in Old Norse.

Pirates and Their Flags: The Jolly Roger and the Golden Age of Piracy

From the portrayal of piracy in popular culture, whether based on fact, fiction, romanticised legend, (from evil antagonist to anti-hero to loveable rogue) or a combination of all of these, we have inherited a set of images conjured up in the mind's eye when we think of pirates, the wooden leg, the parrot perched on the shoulder, the eyepatch, the stylised accent from the south west of England, and also the Jolly Roger or the Skull & Crossbones, a powerful image of mortality whose origins can be traced as far back as the Late Middle Ages.

The use of these symbols by pirates on their flags was designed to strike fear into their prey and encourage them to surrender without a fight. They were also a form of brand identity that would carry with them the power of the reputation that preceded them.

The fact that the Jolly Roger or Skull & Crossbones has been adopted by various military and sports teams around the world, and also as an internationally recognised symbol of danger or poison is testament to the effectiveness of this image. This book examines the origin and evolution of these flags and their common themes and variations, with 67 flags in full colour over 80 pages.

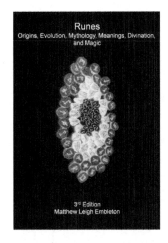

Runes (*English Edition*): Origins, Evolution, Mythology, Meanings, Divination, and Magic

Runes are a fascinating example of the ingenuity of language, communication, and symbolic meaning.

They show us human nature's attempt to use them as tools of expression, a divinatory means to understand the forces that exist all around us that shape our lives, and our attempts to influence these forces by signifying our intentions to the divine and the universe.

Unfortunately like all writing systems and symbols at some time or another in history, they have been misused by a minority in a way that goes against their original meaning and creates misunderstanding in public consciousness about what these symbols really mean, who uses them, and why.

It is the aim of this book to provide the bigger picture about where these symbols have come from, how they have developed, how they have been used, and how their use has evolved over two thousand years.

Runor (*Swedish Edition*): Utspridning, Utveckling, Mytologi, Betydelser, Spådom och Magi

Runor är ett fascinerande exempel på uppfinningsrikedomen för språk, kommunikation och symbolisk betydelse.

De visar oss den mänskliga naturens försök att använda dem som uttrycksverktyg, ett gudomligt sätt att förstå krafterna som finns runt omkring oss som formar våra liv och våra försök att påverka dessa krafter genom att beteckna våra avsikter till det gudomliga och universum.

Tyvärr, liksom alla skrivsystem och symboler på en eller annan tid i historien, har de missbrukats av en minoritet på ett sätt som strider mot deras ursprungliga betydelse och skapar missförstånd i det offentliga medvetandet om vad dessa symboler verkligen betyder, vem som använder dem och varför.

Det är syftet med denna bok att ge en större bild av var dessa symboler kommer från, hur de har utvecklats, hur de har använts och hur deras användning har utvecklats under två tusen år.

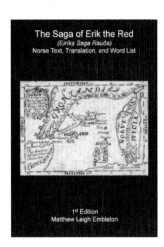

The Saga of Erik the Red (*Eiríks Saga Rauða*): Norse Text, Translation, and Word List

The Saga of Erik the Red (*Eiríks Saga Rauða*) is one of the two Icelandic Sagas which make up the Vínland Sagas (*Vínlandingasögur*) which tell the story of the Norse discovery of North America.

The story includes the events leading up to Erik the Red being banished from Iceland and discovering Greenland. Following the accidental discovery of lands further west of Greenland, there are a number of expeditions to explore and settle these lands.

These stories survived by oral tradition over several centuries before being written down. They are preserved in the *Hauksbók*, and the *Skálholtsbók*.

This book is designed to be of use to anyone studying or with a keen interest in Old Norse or Old Icelandic, clearly showing how these languages work, and the influence of these languages on English. Both Old Norse and Old Icelandic versions are included.

This edition is laid out in three columns, the original text, a literal word-for-word translation, and a modern translation. Also included is a word list with over 1,000 definitions.

Also available in this series: The Saga of the Greenlanders (*Grœnlendinga Saga*), The Vínland Sagas (*Vínlandingasögur*).

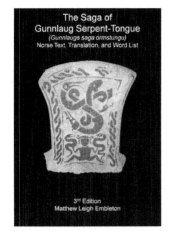

The Saga of Gunnlaug Serpent-Tongue (*Gunnlaugs Saga Ormstungu*): Norse Text, Translation, and Word List

The Saga of Gunnlaug Serpent-Tongue (*Gunnlaugs Saga Ormstungu*) is the story of a promising young man named Gunnlaug who achieves fame for his bravery and poetry in the courts of kings and earls throughout the Norse world.

The story tells of poems praising kings and earls in verses received as gifts, in a culture where gift giving was a well established and important means of settling disputes, showing respect, and gaining favour and honour. However, a prophetic dream foretells the love rivalry and betrayal between Gunnlaugr Ormstunga, Hrafn Önundarson, and Helga the Fair, ending in tragedy.

These stories survived by oral tradition over several centuries before being written down at the beginning of the 14th Century. It is based on two different manuscripts, one from c1270 and the other from c1300, preserved in its complete form in the *Sögubók* (Holm. Perg. 18 4to).

This book is designed to be of use to anyone studying or with a keen interest in Old Norse or Old Icelandic, clearly showing how these languages work, and the influence of these languages on English. Both Old Norse and Old Icelandic versions are included.

This edition is laid out in three columns, the original text, a literal word-for-word translation, and a modern translation. Also included is a word list with over 1,000 definitions.

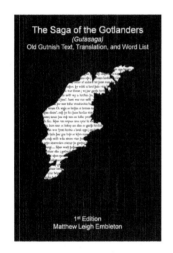

The Saga of the Gotlanders (*Gutasaga*): Old Gutnish Text, Translation, and Word List

The meaning of the word 'saga' (plural: 'sǫgur' or 'sögur') translates as 'that which is said', or more widely: a 'saying', 'statement', 'story', 'tale', or 'narrative'.

The Saga of the Gotlanders gives an account of how Gotland was discovered and populated, their peace treaty with the King of Sweden and annual tribute, and Olaf II of Norway's visit to Gotland, and its conversion to the Christian faith.

What is particularly interesting about the Gutasaga is that it preserves a variety of Old Norse known as Old Gutnish. This variety of Old Norse is believed to have evolved in the 7th century along with Old East Norse and Old West Norse, with Old Gutnish showing enough differences for it to be considered a separate branch of the North Germanic languages all on its own. It also has some similarities with the Gothic language on the East Germanic branch which became extinct around the 8th century.

The Gutasaga is believed to have been written in the 13th century, and makes up most of what we know about Old Gutnish. It survives in a single remaining manuscript, the Codex Holm. B 64, which has been dated to around 1350, and is kept in the National Library of Sweden in Stockholm.

This book is designed to be of use to anyone studying or with a keen interest in Old Gutnish or Old Norse, clearly showing how these languages work, and the influence of these languages on English. This edition is laid out in three columns, the original text, a literal word-for-word translation, and a modern translation. Also included is a word list with over 1,000 definitions.

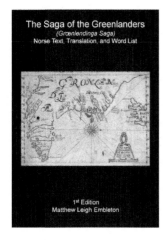

The Saga of the Greenlanders (*Grœnlendinga Saga*): Norse Text, Translation, and Word List

The Saga of the Greenlanders (*Grœnlendinga Saga*) is one of the two Icelandic Sagas which make up the Vínland Sagas (*Vínlandingasögur*) which tell the story of the Norse discovery of North America.

The story includes the events leading up to Erik the Red being banished from Iceland and discovering Greenland. Following the accidental discovery of lands further west of Greenland, there are a number of expeditions to explore and settle these lands.

The story survived by oral tradition over several centuries before being written down in the 13th century. It is preserved in the *Flateyjarbók*.

This book is designed to be of use to anyone studying or with a keen interest in Old Norse or Old Icelandic, clearly showing how these languages work, and the influence of these languages on English. Both Old Norse and Old Icelandic versions are included.

This edition is laid out in three columns, the original text, a literal word-for-word translation, and a modern translation. Also included is a word list with over 1,000 definitions.

Also available in this series: The Saga of Erik the Red (*Eiríks Saga Rauða*) and The Vínland Sagas (*Vínlandingasögur*).

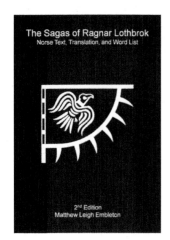

The Sagas of Ragnar Lothbrok (*Ragnarssögur Loðbrókar*): Norse Text, Translation, and Word List

The Sagas of Ragnar Lothbrok (*Ragnarssögur Loðbrókar*) include 'The Saga of Ragnar Lothbrok' (*Ragnars Saga Loðbrókar*) and 'The Tale of Ragnar's Sons' (*Ragnarssona Þáttr*). Also included is The Lay of Kraka (*Krákumál*). The legend of Ragnar Lothbrok, one of the best known heroes of the Viking Age, has been told and re-told in an increasing variety of media.

The story begins with the origins of Ragnar's second wife Aslaug (or Auslag). Then follows the heroic deed of Ragnar taking up the challenge laid down by King Herraud of Götaland, killing a giant serpent belonging to his daughter Thora Fortress-Hart, and winning her hand in marriage. Ragnar's later marriage to Aslaug is followed by the arrival of several sons, who one by one grow strong and plan raiding expeditions of their own.

These stories survived by oral tradition over several centuries before being written down. They are preserved in the *Hauksbók*, and the manuscript NKS (1824b) 4to in Copenhagen, Denmark.

This book is designed to be of use to anyone studying or with a keen interest in Old Norse or Old Icelandic, clearly showing how these languages work, and the influence of these languages on English.

This edition is laid out in three columns, the original text, a literal word-for-word translation, and a modern translation. Also included is a word list with over 1,000 definitions.

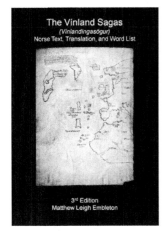

The Vínland Sagas (*Vínlandingasögur*): Norse Text, Translation, and Word List
The Vínland Sagas (*Vínlandingasögur*) contain two Sagas, The Saga of the Greenlanders (*Grœnlendinga Saga*), and The Saga of Erik the Red (*Eiríks Saga Rauða*) which tell the story of the Norse discovery of North America.

The story includes the events leading up to Erik the Red being banished from Iceland and discovering Greenland. Following the accidental discovery of lands further west of Greenland, there are a number of expeditions to explore and settle these lands.

These stories survived by oral tradition over several centuries before being written down in the 13th Century. They are preserved in the *Hauksbók*, the *Skálholtsbók*, and the *Flateyjarbók*.

This book is designed to be of use to anyone studying or with a keen interest in Old Norse or Old Icelandic, clearly showing how these languages work, and the influence of these languages on English. Both Old Norse and Old Icelandic versions are included.

This edition is laid out in three columns, the original text, a literal word-for-word translation, and a modern translation. Also included is a word list with over 1,000 definitions.

Also available in this series: The Saga of Erik the Red (*Eiríks Saga Rauða*), and The Saga of the Greenlanders (*Grœnlendinga Saga*).

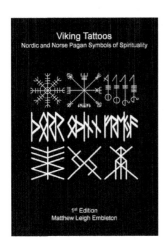

Viking Tattoos: Nordic and Norse Pagan Symbols of Spirituality
In recent decades popular culture has rediscovered the Viking Age and North Germanic Paganism with fresh eyes. From the pirates and sea raiders known as Vikings, to the fierce warriors called Berserkers, and the wider Norse or Nordic people as a whole, symbols played an important role in daily life and spirituality. These symbols were used in many different ways, including writing, divination, recording events, marking and indicating ownership of personal items, and talismanic protection, strength, and luck.

Today we find these symbols visually eye catching and their meanings fascinating. People all over the world are finding meaning in these symbols that resonate with their personality, identity, and spiritual beliefs. Each of these symbols is a visual representation of a thought or an idea, from a single line to an ever increasingly complex symmetry of lines, circles, intersecting lines, and bold striking angles.

Perhaps one of the most popular of these symbols is the Vegvísir, one of the many Galdrastafir (praying or chanting staves) that appeared in Iceland after its settlement by Norse people in the late 9th centuy, but there are many more.

Preserved manuscripts contain a wealth of these magical symbols drawn by hand in personal hand books or grimoires. In some cases there are accompanying sentences explaining their meanings and instruction on their use, and in many cases the very name of the symbol told them all they needed to know, with their uses open to interpretation.

The magic of the Norse people worked because they believed that it worked. They believed in the process of signalling and communicating their intentions and desirable outcomes to the forces around them, projecting them into the universe, and having the confidence and belief to make things happen.

The aim of this book is to explore these symbols and present them to the reader for their consideration as ideas for tattoos or symbols for personal talismanic magic.